THE LEGACY & THE TESTAMENT

Books by Louis Simpson

Poetry
The Arrivistes: Poems 1940-49
Good News of Death and Other Poems
A Dream of Governors
At the End of the Open Road
Selected Poems
Adventures of the Letter I
Searching for the Ox
Caviare at the Funeral
The Best Hour of the Night
People Live Here: Selected Poems 1949-83
Collected Poems
In the Room We Share
Jamaica Poems
There You Are
Nombres et poussière

Literary Criticism
James Hogg: A Critical Study
Three on the Tower: The Lives and Works of Ezra Pound, T. S. Eliot and William Carlos Williams
A Revolution in Taste: Studies of Dylan Thomas, Allen Ginsberg, Sylvia Plath and Robert Lowell
A Company of Poets
The Character of the Poet
Ships Going into the Blue

Other
Riverside Drive (novel)
An Introduction to Poetry
North of Jamaica (autobiography)
Selected Prose
The King My Father's Wreck (memoirs)
Modern Poets of France: A Bilingual Anthology

The Legacy &
The Testament

by François Villon

Translated by Louis Simpson

Story Line Press
Ashland, Oregon

Published by Story Line Press. Three Oaks Farm, PO Box 1240, Ashland, Oregon 97520-0055

Cover drawing by Don Resnick
Book design by Lysa McDowell
Composition by Wellstone Publications

Library of Congress Cataloging-in-Publication Data

Villon, François, b. 1431.
   [Lais, English]
   The legacy ; & The testament / by François Villon ; translated by Louis Simpson.
     p. cm.
   Includes bibliographical references.
   ISBN 1-58654-001-7 (alk. paper) — ISBN 1-885266-99-5 (pbk. : alk. paper)
     I. Title: Legacy ; & The testament. II. Title: Legacy ; and The testament. III.
Simpson, Louis Aston Marantz, 1923- IV. Villon, François, b. 1431. Grant
testament. English. V. Title: Testament. VI. Title.

PQ1590.E5 S56 2000
84'.2—dc21   00-44549

Item: I leave to Matthew, Anne,
And Anthony, a love of life
And books well written, equally.

Contents

Preface

Villon was born in 1431. His father's name was Montcorbier, from a village of that name in the province of Bourbonnais, and there was a noble Bourbon family named Montcorbier, but there is no evidence that the poet's father was related to them. Villon says,

> Poverty tracks us. You may trace
> On tombs a long line coming down,
> Of souls who lie in God's embrace.
> No scepters there, and not a crown.

A number of Bourbonnais settled in Paris following the marriage of Charles V to Jeanne de Bourbon. The poet's mother lived near the royal palace. It is possible that his father was descended from a servant of the queen.

In 1431 Paris was under domination by the English. They had a fearful reputation—it was said that they would cut the throat of anyone they caught outside the city walls. Five years later the English left. There was a procession of thanksgiving for deliverance, and Charles VII, "Charles the Good," entered Paris.

These were years of great hardship. Bands of brigands roamed the city. They seized children and carried them off and kept them in cages so that their parents would pay a ransom. One brigand would throw children that were not ransomed into the fire.

People died of hunger and cold. There was a terrible winter—snow fell for forty days. Wolves were in the streets—they ate the dogs and attacked women and children. There was a ferocious wolf without a tail. He was given a name, Courtaul, Short Tail, and was regarded as a brigand of the forest or ruthless captain. Those who were going into the fields were warned, "Beware of Courtaul."

There was a clergyman named Guillaume de Villon living in the cloister of Saint-Benoît-le-Bétourné. One day a poor woman from the quarter of the Celestins, across the Seine, brought him her little boy whose name was François. Cross over to the Left Bank, walk up rue Saint-Jacques, and when you get to the alley of Saint-Jean-de-Jerusalem you'll see at the end a little old church. That's Saint-Benoît-le-Bétourné where you'll find the cloister.

She was an illiterate but devoutly religious woman, apparently related to Guillaume de Villon. She presented her child to him, and Master Villon adopted François, gave him his name, and brought him up. François' adoptive father treated him with great kindness—the poet would say that Guillaume de Villon was his "more than father." Instead of starving as many children did, and running wild in the streets, François would be educated. "Without doubt, the wise Master Guillaume found it easy to give him his first lessons . . . he taught him the *Donat* and the *Doctrinal* of Alexandre de Villedieu, that is to say, Latin grammar and syntax."[1]

In 1439, after a long, drawn out case at law in which Master Guillaume argued against another contender for the position, Parliament appointed him chaplain of Notre-Dame de Gentilly. He continued to live in the cloister of Saint-Benoît. He became a respected professor of law, obtained properties, and was on familiar terms with men who were powers in the land. The boy who followed in the footsteps of his adoptive father could look forward, one day, to being rich.

In *The Legacy* Villon bequeaths his "tents and pavilion" to Guillaume de Villon. But he doesn't have tents and a pavilion—he doesn't seem to have anything but the clothes on his back. He also says that he is leaving Guillaume de Villon his reputation, to be added to his greater reputation. The reputation of François Villon could only be an embarrassment to the respected chaplain and professor of law.

In *The Testament* he acknowledges the kindness of his adoptive father. But this is ambiguous:

> Item: to my more than father,
> Master Guillaume de Villon,
> Who has been gentler than a mother

---

1. Pierre Champion, *François Villon: Sa Vie et Son Temps I* (Paris: Librairie Honoré Champion, 1967), 30.

With a misbehaving little son...
He got me out of scrapes, and this one
Isn't making him happy. On my knees
I implore him not to take this on.
Let me have all the joy of it, please!

Perhaps it is better to have a real father than one, however kind,
who is more than a father. Such kindness may be oppressive, take all
the joy out of life.

Villon's natural father, Montcorbier, lived to old age. The poet's
only mention of him is respectful:

My father is dead, and lies below
May God keep his soul!

All that is known about Montcorbier is that he was a poor man—
poverty defines him. It seems that François saw himself as standing
in the line of his descent. He turned his back on the advantages
offered by his position as Guillaume de Villon's adopted son, as
though being adopted were an insult to his father that he was going
to avenge.

Besides, he was not cut out for a scholar—as he tells us, he didn't
read much. The boy with a bright future neglected his studies. There
are references to the Bible in his poems, Greek myths, and Roman
authors, but he didn't check his references. At the university he fell
in with bad company: he was one of the students who frequented
the taverns and whores, who gambled, and who sang in the street at
night, keeping decent people awake.

He killed a man in a street fight. Philippe Sermoise came at him
with a dagger, and he laid him out with a stone. He protests that he
was innocent—he would have claimed that he acted in self-defense.
He was let off lightly, only banished from Paris, and was absent for
four years. He appealed for remission of the sentence and was per-
mitted by "royal clemency" to return. The letters of remission are
dated in January, 1456.

A robbery of *écus* from the strongbox at the College of Navarre at
Christmas of that year was not settled so easily. He was suspected of
having taken part in the crime, and found it expedient to leave Paris

again and wander in the provinces. Five years would pass before he returned. This time he had to remain in hiding. He had been implicated in the robbery and was wanted for questioning.

There is a second bequest to Guillaume de Villon in *The Testament*, leaving him the *Romance of the Farting Devil*, a poem Villon is said to have written in his student days. If he did write such a poem, it would have had to do with the students' carrying off a big stone named the Farting Devil that belonged to a Mademoiselle de Bruyères. This was one of the incidents that brought the students into conflict with the police. The bequest of this "romance" will remind Guillaume de Villon of his adopted son's outrageous behavior. It is a parting shot.

Very few poets have had a life as active as Villon's, so much experience of the world, especially the lower depths. But *The Legacy* and *The Testament* are not autobiography. Villon gives the narrator, the "I" of the poems, his name, and the narrator refers to things that have happened to him, but he does not give us the facts, only his afterthoughts. There are times when, as David Mus says, we have to go by "the facts of the style."[2]

The narrator leaves us in the dark about two crucial events. In *Le Lais* he says that he was questioned about his involvement in a crime... which he does not describe. In *Le Testament* he tells us that he was imprisoned at Mehun, and that he was starved and beaten... but not why.

From legal and church records we know that a François Villon studied at the University of Paris, and that he killed a man in a street fight. We know that he took part in the robbery of the College of Navarre; that he went on the road and lived rough; that he associated with thieves. The voice in the poems is the voice of this man—with variations.

At the beginning of *Le Lais* he is writing a parody of the literature of courtly love. Mus says that the situation described in these pages is a fiction. The "dungeon of love" in which the narrator says he was

---

2. David Mus, *La Poétique de François Villon* (Paris: Librairie Armand Colin, 1967; Editions Champ Villon, 1992).

imprisoned is, in fact, the old style of the poetry of courtly love from which he has to escape. The woman who he says betrayed him is fictional. The parody of scholastic jargon with which *Le Lais* concludes is not merely the comic turn that readers have taken it to be—Villon is clearing the ground for the new kind of poetry he intends to write.

I find in the opening pages of *Le Lais* something more than parody—a real fear of imprisonment. And it seems real to me when he says that his life is in danger. Yes, he is parodying an outworn, affected style of writing, but the parody is not only a literary exercise, it refers to an actual situation.

The man is the style. The author of *Le Lais* and *Le Testament* made fiction of his life, but it was no fiction when he was imprisoned at Mehun-sur-Loire, put in chains, tortured, and kept alive on bread and water. His style was shaped in the light of his experience. How could it not have been?

But our impressions as we read cannot always be trusted. The ballade about "the snows of yesterday" was read by generations as a lament for women who were as beautiful as the snow that, alas, vanishes. Mus points out that in the Middle Ages snow was not associated with beauty—it came in winter, the dreaded time of cold and hunger, when wolves were in the streets. How is it that we could not see this for ourselves? We simply did not know enough.

Two women named in the first stanza, Flora and Thais, were beautiful (Echo was too beautiful to be human). The other women in the ballade were not famous for their beauty. Heloise was known for her learning. Blanche de Bourgogne, the wife of Charles IV, was condemned for adultery and repudiated by her husband. Bertha Bigfoot may be either the wife of Pépin le Bref and mother of Charlemagne, or King Robert's wife who was punished by God for an incestuous marriage, or both—for in folklore names and characters were often conflated. Bertha gave birth to a son with the head and neck of a goose, and her right foot was changed into the foot of a goose. A lament for vanished beauties? Hardly. Other of the women were noted for other reasons. Joan of Arc would be canonized, and the list culminates with the Virgin Mary.

The key to the poem is the story of the Queen of France who arranged to have Buridan, a professor at the university, "bagged and dropped in the Seine." (The story must have been handed down by students.) The Queen disposed of her lovers in this fashion. The fifteenth-century reader would have known that "sack" referred to female genitalia. Buridan's being put in a sack was sexual intercourse. Buridan was to be drowned, but he survived by a ruse—and when snow melts it turns to water, which pours into rivers, which fertilize the land.

What is being described here is metamorphosis, the changing of the seasons and regeneration. Woman is associated with fluidity and regeneration. (Echo's beauty was reflected in water, and there was talk of Joan of Arc's bones having been put in the Seine.) No matter how often the Prince asks where the snows have gone, *ubi sunt*, he will receive the same answer. The females in the poem, and Buridan, the male, are included in the permanent, changing life of Nature. We are all carried away by "the river of fertile change."

Many do not find this consoling. What becomes of the individual? Are we to be nothing more than a butterfly or a leaf of grass? Mus comments: "It is precisely in stanzas 7 to 11, which are intended to evoke the world of Nature, that Villon is careful to distinguish between his weak natural body, with its five senses, in the process of disappearing, and his "sense," his understanding, which comes to him from God and in no way shares the "weakness" of his natural prison:

> Since it seems I am so poor
> In worldly goods, not my body,
> And still have all the power
> Of such sense as God gave me,
> For I borrowed it from nobody..."[3]

This is a very different reading of the ballade of "the snows of yesterday" than the one it used to get. Would a reader today arrive at such understanding without the assistance of the critic? I do not think so. But it is rare for Villon's poetry to have to be explained. Lyric poetry is dramatic, it works immediately upon our senses, and

---

3. Mus 280.

none more forcefully than the poetry of Villon. In translating these poems I have tried to make the drama as clear, the tone of his voice, his meaning, as clear as he makes it: "the voice at once incisive and spontaneous, frank and tricky, which for us *is* Villon."[4]

Four hundred years after Villon, Baudelaire will say that the artist who is gifted with an active imagination is looking for something that he, Baudelaire, would call "modernity." It is a matter of disengaging from the fashion of the moment what it may contain of poetry, extracting the eternal from the transitory. The artist who aims to understand "the character of present beauty" does not have the right to hold the transitory and fugitive in contempt—the mysterious beauty that human life expresses involuntarily as it passes must be extracted. "Nearly all our originality," Baudelaire concludes, "comes from the stamp that the present impresses on our sensations."

Villon anticipates the impressionism that will be practiced by nineteenth and twentieth century artists and writers. Ford Maddox Ford described the method as making the reader think that he is witnessing something real, passing through an experience. Villon's "natural" voice does this—he dramatizes his thoughts as well as any modernist:

> True! I'm against love. I despise it,
> Defy it in fire and in blood.
> I can pick up my fiddle by the exit
> As I leave. She wishes I would.
> I can go straight to hell. Understood?
> What, they ask, am I waiting for?
> All right, I'm going. This time for good.
> I won't be coming back any more.

Poetry is always in the avant-garde because it aims, as Baudelaire said, to "extract the eternal from the transitory."

Villon is a master of narrative—the episode of Alexander and the pirate, for example. You hear the tone of voice, *de haut en bas,* as

---

4. Mus 140.

Alexander asks, "Why / Do you live by piracy?" What purpose can there be in asking this question except to humiliate Diomedes? The pirate answers to the point: "If I had your arms, believe me, / I'd be an emperor like you," and gives Alexander a brief lecture on fate: we are not responsible for our bad habits—we are the product of our conditioning. Alexander is persuaded and says, "I'll change your fate." He releases the pirate and sets him up for life.

This was an old story, told by the fourth-century writer Julius Valerius, but Villon adds a touch that is all his own. Not only does Diomedes give up piracy, he gives up another bad habit—from that day on he stops swearing. So the poet sends up the moral endings of poems. Villon does not lay on his irony with a shovel—he writes for the understanding reader.

He can render a character unforgettably—the Helmet Maker as she tells how beautiful she used to be, and how she has come down in the world; Jehan Cotart stumbling drunk in the street, stamping his feet like an old man, with a big bump on his forehead.

> Is he really dead?
> He took good company so much to heart....
> If you hear a knock when you've gone to bed,
> Let in the soul of the late Jehan Cotart.

Not only individuals—he shows mankind in their occupations and packs: the rich with their sumptuous meals, good wine, big fish, plump fowls, and *flans*—and the man running to wait on them. The ones who have put on religion for expediency, who wear high boots, prayer book in hand: "The different things men have to do!"

There are themes running through *Le Lais* and *Le Testament*. The fate that makes one person rich and another poor —which raises questions about justice, the kind that has placed a sadist like Bishop d'Aussigny in a position of power. It calls into question the nature of the church. It is possible, it seems, for a church to become corrupt.

The theme dearest to François is the nature of love—I say the dearest because he describes himself, more than once, as a "martyr of love." This kind of language, from the literature of courtly love, was already outdated and being parodied when Villon wrote *Le Lais*. He discarded the style and found his own, natural way of dealing with the subject. In the ballade about "the snows of yesterday" he presents woman as the regenerative principle. Men have their place in the process by which children are made and the race continues. But he is not always so high-minded about sex—he speaks as one who is on intimate terms with shopgirls and prostitutes. They confide in him about their affairs, and at the end we find him living in "love's mansion," that is, a brothel.

But never, it seems, has poor Villon been loved:

> Whenever I would talk to her
> She didn't agree or disagree,
> But seemed willingly to hear.
> And what's more, she would let me
> Come close and whisper. . . .

I see Swann talking to Odette during an evening at Madame Verdurin's. Is this not the way she flattered Swann, with an intimacy that set them apart from the other people in the room? And one can see how she might have spoken of him later behind his back.

> And so she
> Strung me along, led by the nose,
> Telling her everything . . . to be
> Made a fool of later, as she chose.

Not many people in those days expected to live to old age. When Villon was a child, 15,000 in Paris died of a smallpox epidemic. Justice was rough, and the bodies of the hanged remained on gibbets for all to see. Skulls and bones were on display in cemeteries. People came to gaze at them as today you might visit a museum of natural history.

The Testament anticipates the photographs of such things that Nadar would make in the nineteenth century when the dead were uprooted and heaped in ossuaries to make way for the boulevards of Baron Haussmann. No one who has seen those photographs is likely to forget them. Villon's meditation on the subject is also memorable:

When I think of all the skulls
In charnel houses, piled in rows...

And those heads once owned great lands,
And bowed and scraped to one another,
And gave other heads commands,
Who hastened to obey, in fear...

In a mural in the Campo Santo at Pisa, beautiful people are riding past open coffins that show bodies in progressive stages of corruption. The riders seem mildly curious, but they aren't going to change their ways. Their fanciful clothes, the bells on their horses, show a contempt for worms and putrefying flesh. In the midst of death we are in life.

There is a fine *joie de vivre* in Villon's pictures of the age. To be poor was his hell, as he says in the lines against Gontier, but he doesn't whine about it, that is, not for long. He has seen the arrogance of the rich and powerful, and he wants what he has written about them to stand, but he also knows himself. He'd be on horseback too if he could, and have one of those proud, beautiful ladies for his mistress. He'd like to be in a warm room, making love to My Lady Sidoine, but he's living in a brothel, and he has Grosse Margot. He doesn't blame this on society, "the system."

                                              this life is mine.
                    I'm rotten, this rotten woman suits me fine...
                    We love filth, and so filth follows us.
                    We fly from honor, and honor abhors us...

Rousseau would claim to be the first to show a man's true character in all its nakedness, but in comparison with Villon, Rousseau is a poseur. There is nothing self-adulatory, nothing to brag about in what Villon writes of his life.

There is one aspect of that life, however, that he does not write about openly, the criminal side. Like a mischievous boy he hints at it: when he assigns a house to be entered on a certain day, what does he mean but burglary? He winks at the reader... he thinks that being a thief is an attractive trait.

On this subject, if no other, he deludes himself. Strange that the poet who warned young men vividly against the bite of the gallows should have been so willing to risk it for himself! He may actually have believed that he was as innocent as he claimed to be, like the pirate Diomedes who blamed his bad habits on fate. A belief like that could put you in prison—it could get you hanged.

But he has a sense of connection with a power greater than the powers of the world. Speaking of his mother he says that he has no castle or fortress to leave her—his only refuge has been Our Lady, and this is the only refuge she will have. In the ballade he writes for her she talks to the Mother of God, woman to woman. The faith of his mother, *foy*, in the sense of an unbreakable contract, is his own. His confidence that he has such a contract enables him to shrug off his unlucky, disreputable character:

> since I
> Have had some fun, and will again—
> I don't much mind having to die.

Poor Villon! He leaves the stage like a clown . . . and joins in the laughter of the audience:

> He was driven from love's mansion
> By hate. I say this truthfully,
> From here as far as Roussillon
> There wasn't a bush that didn't have on
> A bit of rag stained with his gore.

The remark about a bush and a bit of rag has an erotic meaning. Exhausted though he was, a martyr to love, even as he lay dying François was so inclined.

L. S.

The Text

The text, as has become traditional, is that of the edition of Auguste Longnon, revised by Lucien Foulet and in accord with the edition of Louis Thuasne.

THE LEGACY &
THE TESTAMENT

LE LAIS

L'an quatre cens cinquante six,
Je, Françoys Villon, escollier,
Considerant, de sens rassis,
Le frain aux dens, franc au collier,
Qu'on doit ses oeuvres conseillier,
Comme Vegece le raconte,
Sage Rommain, grant conseillier,
Ou autrement on se mesconte...

En ce temps que j'ay dit devant,
Sur le Noel, morte saison,
Que les loups se vivent de vent
Et qu'on se tient en sa maison,
Pour le frimas, pres du tison,
Me vint ung vouloir de brisier
La tres amoureuse prison
Qui souloit mon cuer debrisier.

Je le feis en telle façon,
Voyant celle devant mes yeulx
Consentant a ma desfaçon,
Sans ce que ja luy en fust mieulx;
Dont je me dueil et plains aux cieulx,
En requerant d'elle venjance
A tous les dieux venerieux,
Et du grief d'amours allejance.

Et se j'ay prins en ma faveur
Ces doulx regars et beaux semblans
De tres decevante saveur
Me trespersans jusques aux flans,
Bien ilz ont vers moy les piez blans
Et me faillent au grant besoing.
Planter me fault autres complans
Et frapper en ung autre coing.

THE LEGACY

In fourteen hundred and fifty-six
I, the scholar, François Villon,
Bit in my teeth, no bites or kicks,
As sound of mind as anyone,
Reviewing all that had been done,
My fieldworks—do not let it wait,
Says Vegetius the Roman,
Or else you will miscalculate—

When Christmas came around once more,
The season when the world is dead,
The frost is thick and hard and hoar
And wolves upon the wind are fed,
I had one idea in my head,
To break out of my prison cell,
The love that for so long had made
My life here on this earth a hell.

I went about it in this fashion:
I saw her standing in plain sight,
Consenting to my execution
Although she could gain nothing by it.
And so I suffer day and night,
And call upon the gods of love
To make her pay, and speed my flight
From this, the darkest dungeon, love.

And if she seemed to favor me
With loving looks and countenance
So that I felt my flesh to be
Pierced through and through as by a lance,
Like horses with white feet, her glance
To me now only means betrayal,
And so I'll see what other chance
In planting to my lot may fall.

Le regart de celle m'a prins
Qui m'a esté felonne et dure:
Sans ce qu'en riens aye mesprins,
Veult et ordonne que j'endure
La mort, et que plus je ne dure;
Si n'y voy secours que fouïr.
Rompre veult la vive souldure,
Sans mes piteux regretz oïr!

Pour obvier a ces dangiers,
Mon mieulx est, ce croy, de fouïr.
Adieu! Je m'en vois a Angiers:
Puis qu'el ne me veult impartir
Sa grace, il me convient partir.
Par elle meurs, les membres sains;
Au fort, je suis amant martir
Du nombre des amoureux sains.

Combien que le depart me soit
Dur, si faut il que je l'eslongne:
Comme mon povre sens conçoit,
Autre que moy est en quelongne,
Dont oncques soret de Boulongne
Ne fut plus alteré d'umeur.
C'est pour moy piteuse besongne:
Dieu en veuille oïr ma clameur!

Et puis que departir me fault,
Et du retour ne suis certain
(Je ne suis homme sans desfault
Ne qu'autre d'acier ne d'estain,
Vivre aux humains est incertain
Et après mort n'y a relaiz,
Je m'en vois en pays loingtain),
Si establis ce present laïz.

I was ensnared and caught by one
Who treats me now with cruelty,
And all for nothing I have done,
Who wishes and ordains for me
Death, that I should cease to be.
Such is the verdict in her face,
No room for bargaining, no plea
For mercy in "this painful case."

Now my very life's in danger,
I must escape at once, and so,
Goodbye! I'm going to Angers:
Without a word from her, I know,
No comfort for me as I go,
Martyred for love. And if I were
A statue standing in a row,
That is how much I mean to her.

To leave without a word of grace…
There is no help, it has to be,
For someone else is in my place—
No herring swimming in the sea
At Boulogne happier than he!
Toilworn and pitiful am I.
May God be merciful to me.
Out of the depths to Him I cry!

And as it seems that I must go,
And my return is far from certain—
I am not without fault, you know,
And am not made of bronze or iron,
And human life can be uncertain,
And I must travel a long way,
And death is such a final curtain—
I'm making out my will today.

Premierement, ou nom du Pere,
Du Filz et du Saint Esperit,
Et de sa glorieuse Mere
Par qui grace riens ne perit,
Je laisse, de par Dieu, mon bruit
A maistre Guillaume Villon,
Qui en l'onneur de son nom bruit,
Mes tentes et mon pavillon.

Item, a celle que j'ai dit,
Qui si durement m'a chassié
Que je suis de joye interdit
Et de tout plaisir dechassié,
Je laisse mon cuer enchassié,
Palle, piteux, mort et transy:
Elle m'a ce mal pourchassié,
Mais Dieu luy en face mercy!

Item, a maistre Ythier Marchant,
Auquel je me sens tres tenu,
Laisse mon branc d'acier tranchant,
Ou a maistre Jehan le Cornu,
Qui est en gaige detenu
Pour ung escot huit solz montant;
Si vueil, selon le contenu,
Qu'on leur livre, en le rachetant.

Item, je laisse a Saint Amant
Le Cheval Blanc, avec *la Mulle*,
Et a Blarru mon dyamant
Et *l'Asne Royé* qui reculle.
Et le decret qui articulle
Omnis utriusque sexus,
Contre la Carmeliste bulle
Laisse aux curez, pour mettre sus.

In the name of the Father, Son,
And Holy Ghost, and by her grace,
The Mother, the resplendent one
To whom there is no hopeless case,
God willing, my good name I place
With Master Guillaume Villon
Whose greater fame may mine embrace,
My tents and my pavilion.

Item: I'm leaving to the one
Who cast me off so heartlessly
My every joy in life is gone,
No pleasure left that I can see,
A heart encased in misery,
Pale, bloodless, murdered, and enshrined,
Such evil she has done to me...
May God forgive her wicked mind!

Item: to Master Ythier Marchant,
My good friend, if he has eight sous
To pay the bar tab—if he can't,
I leave to Jehan le Cornu—
My sword that's sharp and good as new
But resting uselessly in jail.
I'm hereby authorizing you
To set it free. Just go the bail.

Item: I leave to Saint Amant
The *White Horse* tavern and *She-Mule;*
And to Blarru my diamond
And *Zebra* that appears to pull
Backward; and the whole decretal,
Omnis utriusque sexus,
Against Carmelites and their bull,
To the priests. Enforce it for us.

Et a maistre Robert Valee,
Povre clerjot en Parlement,
Qui n'entent ne mont ne vallee,
J'ordonne principalement
Qu'on luy baille legierement
Mes brayes, estans aux *Trumillieres*,
Pour coeffer plus honnestement
S'amye Jehanne de Millieres.

Pour ce qu'il est de lieu honneste,
Fault qu'il soit mieulx recompensé,
Car Saint Esperit l'admoneste,
Obstant ce qu'il est insensé;
Pour ce, je me suis pourpensé
Qu'on lui baille l'Art de Memoire
A recouvrer sur Maupensé,
Puis qu'il n'a sens ne qu'une aulmoire.

Item, pour assigner la vie
Du dessusdit maistre Robert,
(Pour Dieu, n'y ayez point d'envie!)
Mes parens, vendez mon haubert,
Et que l'argent, ou la plus part,
Soit emploié, dedans ces Pasques,
A acheter a ce poupart
Une fenestre emprès Saint Jaques.

Item, laisse et donne en pur don
Mes gans et ma hucque de soye
A mon amy Jacques Cardon,
Le glan aussi d'une saulsoye,
Et tous les jours une grasse oye
Et ung chappon de haulte gresse,
Dix muys de vins blanc comme croye,
Et deux procès, que trop n'engresse.

Item: I leave to Robert Valée,
Poor little clerk in Parliament
Who doesn't know hill from valley,
The pants I left when last I went
Into the *Greaves* on pleasure bent.
The ones his girlfriend ought to wear...
The way he keeps her is indecent,
I mean Jehanne de Millieres.

He comes of a good family,
Decent, hard working, country bred,
And so his wages ought to be
Better, the Holy Ghost has said,
Though he's a fool. So I've decided
To leave my *Art of Memory*
To him, to fill his wooden head
That right now is standing empty.

Item: to provide a lunch pail
For the said Master Valée,
Kinsmen, sell my coat of mail
(Now don't all give way to envy!)
And by Easter use the money,
Or greater part, to buy a stall
For a scribe and secretary
At Saint Jacques right beneath the wall.

Item: as a pure bequest,
I leave my good friend Jacques Cardon
My gloves and cape, silk, of the best,
Also the acorn, a rare one
From a willow; a plump capon;
Every day a goose for dinner,
Wine, chalk-white, by the gallon,
And two lawsuits to make him thinner.

Item, je laisse a ce noble homme,
Regnier de Montigny, troys chiens;
Aussi a Jehan Raguier la somme
De cent frans, prins sur tous mes biens.
Mais quoy? Je n'y comprens en riens
Ce que je pourray acquerir;
On ne doit trop prendre des siens,
Ne son amy trop surquerir.

Item, au seigneur de Grigny
Laisse la garde de Nijon,
Et six chiens plus qu'a Montigny,
Vicestre, chastel et donjon;
Et a ce malostru chanjon,
Mouton, qui le tient en procès,
Laisse trois coups d'ung escourjon,
Et couchier, paix et aise, es ceps.

Et a maistre Jaques Raguier
Laisse l'Abruvouër Popin,
Perches, poussins au blanc mengier,
Tousjours le chois d'ung bon loppin,
Le trou de *la Pomme de Pin,*
Clos et couvert, au feu la plante,
Emmailloté en jacoppin;
Et qui voudra planter, si plante.

Item, a maistre Jehan Mautaint
Et a maistre Pierre Basanier,
Le gré du seigneur qui attaint
Troubles, forfaiz, sans espargnier;
Et a mon procureur Fournier,
Bonnetz cours, chausses semelees,
Taillees sur mon cordouannier,
Pour porter durant ces gelees.

Item: to Regnier de Montigny
Three dogs. A hundred francs in sum
To Jehan Raguier tax free.
But what's the matter? Why so glum?
That's cash in hand, not kingdom come.
There are times when one has to live
Thriftily, to provide for some,
And friends don't ask what friends can't give.

Item: to Seigneur de Grigny
I leave the ward of Nigeon,
Six dogs more than Montigny,
And Bicêtre, tower and dungeon.
To that devil's whelp, Mouton,
Who's taking him to court, I will
The bastonade, three blows, and iron
Around each leg to keep him still.

Item: I leave Jacques Raguier
The old Popin watering place;
Good food and drink there every day,
Perch, pullet with white sauce, or dace;
The Pine Cone Saddle Bar in case
You'd like to sit there, snug and warm,
And if you want a pretty face
To plant with, upstairs it's the farm!

Item: the favor of their lord
To Jehan Mautaint and Pierre
Basanier, him whose keen sword
Strikes crime, riot, and does not spare.
And may Fournier my lawyer wear
Close nightcaps and the fitted slippers
My shoemaker makes with a flair
For cold days, toe and finger nippers.

Item, a Jehan Trouvé, bouchier,
Laisse *le Mouton* franc et tendre,
Et ung tacon pour esmouchier
Le Beuf Couronné qu'on veult vendre,
Et *la Vache:* qui pourra prendre
Le vilain qui la trousse au col,
S'il ne la rent, qu'on le puist pendre
Et estrangler d'ung bon licol!

Item, au Chevalier de Guet,
Le Hëaulme luy establis;
Et aux pietons qui vont d'aguet
Tastonnant par ces establis,
Je leur laisse deux beaux rubis,
La Lanterne a la Pierre au Let.
Voire, mais j'auray *les Troys Lis*,
S'ilz me mainent en Chastellet.

Item, a Perrenet Marchant,
Qu'on dit le Bastart de la Barre,
Pour ce qu'il est tres bon marchant,
Luy laisse trois gluyons de fuerre
Pour estendre dessus la terre
A faire l'amoureux mestier,
Ou il luy fauldra sa vie querre,
Car il ne scet autre mestier.

Item, au Loup et a Cholet
Je laisse a la fois ung canart
Prins sur les murs, comme on souloit,
Envers les fossez, sur le tart,
Et a chascun ung grant tabart
De cordelier jusques aux piez,
Busche, charbon et poix au lart,
Et mes houseaulx sans avantpiez.

Item: the butcher, Jehan Trouvé,
I leave *The Sheep*, so fat and tender.
Get rid of the flies...someone may
Buy *The Crowned Ox*. Have my swatter.
And do you think I could forget her,
The Cow? I most devoutly hope
The thief who is seen running with her
Across his back hangs with his rope.

Item: the Captain of the Watch
I leave *The Helmet* he must show;
And to his men, so keen to catch
Housebreakers, treading on tiptoe,
Two rubies with a lovely glow,
And *The Lantern* in Pierre au Let.
But I'll take *Three Lilies* when I go
If they send me to the Châtelet.

Item: to Perrenet Marchant,
With a bar sinister, it's said,
Because he is a leading merchant,
Three bales of straw that may be spread
To make a comfortable bed
For lovers on the cold, hard ground,
Or try to find some other trade,
But this is the only one he's found.

Item: to both Loup and Cholet,
I leave a duck caught on the wall
Close to the moat, in the old way,
When it's getting late. That's not all:
To each, one of those cloaks that fall
Down to the feet, and good suppers,
Peas, porkfat, firewood and coal,
And my boots that have no uppers.

De rechief, je laisse, en pitié,
A trois petis enfans tous nus
Nommez en ce present traictié,
Povres orphelins impourveus,
Tous deschaussiez, tous despourveus
Et desnuez comme le ver;
J'ordonne qu'ilz soient pourveus,
Au moins pour passer cest yver:

Premierement, Colin Laurens,
Girart Gossouyn et Jehan Marceau,
Despourveus de biens, de parens,
Qui n'ont vaillant l'ance d'ung seau,
Chascun de mes biens ung fesseau,
Ou quatre blans, s'ilz l'ayment mieulx.
Ilz mangeront maint bon morceau,
Les enfans, quant je seray vieulx!

Item, ma nominacion,
Que j'ay de l'Université,
Laisse par resignacion
Pour seclurre d'aversité
Povres clers de ceste cité
Soubz cest *intendit* contenus;
Charité m'y a incité,
Et Nature, les voiant nus:

C'est maistre Guillaume Cotin
Et maistre Thibault de Victry,
Deux povres clers, parlans latin,
Paisibles enfans, sans estry,
Humbles, bien chantans au lectry;
Je leurs laisse cens recevoir
Sur la maison Guillot Gueuldry,
En attendant de mieulx avoir.

Also there are the little ones
Whom I shall straightway designate...
Completely naked, three orphans
In a most pitiable state,
Naked as a worm. This can't wait,
They have to be provided for
With shoes and clothing. See to it,
At least see them through this winter.

First, I leave to Colin Laurens,
Girart Gossouyn and Jehan Marceau,
Deprived of all, with no parents,
And not a bucket strap to show,
A part of my goods, divided so,
Or four *blancs* if that's what appeals.
When I am an old man, I know
The children will have hearty meals.

Item: the Master of the Arts,
Bestowed by blockheads equally
On scholars and—what rhymes with Arts?—
Was never any use to me.
Auction it off and give the money
To the poor clerks named below.
This I am doing out of pity
On seeing them denuded so.

These are Master Guillaume Cotin
And Master Thibault de Victry,
Two poor clerks who speak Latin,
Peaceful and humble as could be,
Tuneful in church as do-re-mi.
I leave them what the butcher pays
In rent—I mean Guillot Gueuldry,
Until they can see better days.

Item, et j'adjoings a la crosse
Celle de la rue Saint Anthoine,
Ou ung billart de quoy on crosse,
Et tous les jours plain pot de Saine;
Aux pijons qui sont en l'essoine,
Enserrez soubz trappe volliere,
Mon mirouër bel et ydoine
Et la grace de la geolliere.

Item, je laisse aux hospitaux
Mes chassiz tissus d'arigniee,
Et aux gisans soubz les estaux,
Chascun sur l'oeil une grongniee,
Trembler a chiere renfrongniee,
Megres, velus et morfondus,
Chausses courtes, robe rongniee,
Gelez, murdris et enfondus.

Item, je laisse a mon barbier
Les rongneures de mes cheveulx,
Plainement et sans destourbier;
Au savetier mes souliers vieulx,
Et au freppier mes habitz tieulx
Que, quant du tout je les delaisse,
Pour moins qu'ilz ne cousterent neufz
Charitablement je leur laisse.

Item, je laisse aux Mendians,
Aux Filles Dieu et aux Beguines,
Savoureux morceaulx et frians,
Flaons, chappons et grasses gelines,
Et puis preschier les Quinze Signes,
Et abatre pain a deux mains,
Carmes chevauchent noz voisines,
Mais cela, ce n'est que du mains.

To their cross I shall add one more:
The cross that's painted in the sign
In rue Saint Anthoine above a door,
Or cross for billiards, and a plain
Pot every day drawn from the Seine.
To pigeons who are locked in jail
I leave my mirror with no stain,
Also the jailer's wife's good will.

I bequeath to all hospitals
Spider webs on dirty windows,
To men who sleep beneath street stalls,
A punch for each, right in the nose.
May they shake when the wind blows,
Their coats too short, their breeches holed,
Soak when it rains, freeze when it snows,
And cough, with a persistent cold.

Item: I bequeath the hair
For which I have no further use
To my barber, free and clear;
To the shoemaker, my old shoes;
And the ragpicker won't refuse
My old clothes. They cost me plenty
When they were new, but still I choose
To give them, out of charity.

Item: I leave the Mendicant,
The Filles Dieu, and the Beguine,
All the good things to eat they want,
Capon, pâté, and fat hen;
To preach on signs appearing when
The world is ending, and beg bread.
Carmelites ride our wives, but then
It doesn't count, or so they've said.

Item, laisse *le Mortier d'Or*
A Jehan, l'espicier, de la Garde,
Une potence de Saint Mor,
Pour faire ung broyer a moustarde.
A celluy qui fist l'avant garde
Pour faire sur moy griefz exploiz,
De par moy saint Anthoine l'arde!
Je ne luy feray autre laiz.

Item, je laisse a Merebeuf
Et a Nicolas de Louvieux,
A chascun l'escaille d'ung oeuf,
Plaine de frans et d'escus vieulx.
Quant au concierge de Gouvieulx,
Pierre de Rousseville, ordonne,
Pour le donner entendre mieulx,
Escus telz que le Prince donne.

Finablement, en escripvant,
Ce soir, seulet, estant en bonne,
Dictant ce laiz et descripvant,
J'oïs la cloche de Serbonne,
Qui tousjours a neuf heures sonne
Le Salut que l'Ange predit;
Si suspendis et y mis bonne
Pour prier comme le cuer dit.

Ce faisant, je m'entroublié,
Non pas par force de vin boire,
Mon esperit comme lié;
Lors je sentis dame Memoire
Reprendre et mettre en son aumoire
Ses especes collateralles,
Oppinative faulce et voire,
Et autres intellectualles.

Item: I leave *The Golden Mortar*
To Jehan, grocer, of the Guard;
One of the crutches of Saint Maur,
A pestle for a pot of mustard.
Spread it then, as thick as lard,
On him who caused my misery.
Burn, Saint Anthony, the bastard!
He'll get no other legacy.

Item: to Merebeuf, and to
Nicolas de Louviers as well,
As many a franc and old *écu*
As can be fitted in a shell.
And all the good *écus* that fell
When the Prince rode by, I will
To one at Gouvieux like a bell
At tax time, Pierre de Rousseville.

This evening as I wrote my will,
Alone, but liking what I wrote,
The Sorbonne bell began to peal.
Nine times the iron clapper smote,
Nine times came ringing from its throat
The promise that the angel made
To save mankind. At the last note
I put my writing down and prayed.

I almost fell asleep right there.
But not from wine—it was as though
I had been shackled to my chair.
And then I watched, as at a show,
Dame Memory placing in a row
Things from the natural sciences,
On shelves. She said that I must know
All of her dependent species.

Et mesmement l'estimative,
Par quoy prospective nous vient,
Similative, formative,
Desquels bien souvent il advient
Que, par leur trouble, homme devient
Fol et lunatique par mois:
Je l'ay leu, se bien m'en souvient,
Et Aristote aucunes fois.

Dont le sensitif s'esveilla
Et esvertua Fantasie,
Qui tous organes resveilla,
Et tint la souvraine partie
En suspens et comme amortie
Par oppression d'oubliance
Qui en moy s'estoit espartie
Pour monstrer des sens l'aliance.

Puis que mon sens fut a repos
Et l'entendement demeslé,
Je cuidé finer mon propos;
Mais mon ancre trouvé gelé
Et mon cierge trouvé soufflé
De feu je n'eusse peu finer;
Si m'endormis, tout emmouflé,
Et ne peus autrement finer.

Fait au temps de ladite date
Par le bien renommé Villon,
Qui ne menjue figue ne date.
Sec et noir comme escouvillon,
Il n'a tente ne pavillon
Qu'il n'ait laissié a ses amis,
Et n'a mais qu'ung peu de billon
Qui sera tantost a fin mis.

I remembered: the estimative
Provides prospective, that provides
The simulative, formative.
And if these channels are denied
The brain overflows like a tide
And drives a man out of his head.
All this, and much more beside,
Said Aristotle, whom I'd read.

But now sensation woke again,
Imagination was relit,
With all the organs that had lain
Dormant and as though decrepit.
The part of me that used to sit
As sovereign had been depressed
And driven out, to show that it,
In my right mind, ruled all the rest.

I had regained my peace of mind,
My brain, it seemed, sound as a bell.
I set to work again, to find
My ink was frozen in the well,
My candle blown out, dark as hell,
No other way to have a light.
And so with mittens on I fell
Asleep, and that was all. Goodnight.

Done on the aforementioned date
By Villon with a reputation
But neither date nor fig to eat.
Who's dry and black and overdone,
Who gave his tents and pavilion,
All that he ever had, to friends.
Now his money is almost gone,
And soon will be. And so it ends.

LE TESTAMENT

En l'an de mon trentiesme aage,
Que toutes mes hontes j'eus beues,
Ne du tout fol, ne du tout sage,
Non obstant maintes peines eues,
Lesquelles j'ay toutes receues
Soubz la main Thibault d'Aussigny...
S'evesque il est, seignant les rues,
Qu'il soit le mien je le regny.

Mon seigneur n'est ne mon evesque,
Soubz luy ne tiens, s'il n'est en friche;
Foy ne luy doy n'hommage avecque,
Je ne suis son serf ne sa biche.
Peu m'a d'une petite miche
Et de froide eaue tout ung esté;
Large ou estroit, moult me fut chiche:
Tel luy soit Dieu qu'il m'a esté!

Et s'aucun me vouloit reprendre
Et dire que je le mauldis,
Non fais, si bien le scet comprendre;
En riens de luy je ne mesdis.
Vecy tout le mal que j'en dis:
S'il m'a esté misericors,
Jhesus, le roy de Paradis,
Tel luy soit a l'ame et au corps!

Et s'esté m'a dur et cruel
Trop plus que cy ne le raconte,
Je vueil que le Dieu eternel
Luy soit donc semblable a ce compte...
Et l'Eglise nous dit et compte
Que prions pour noz ennemis,
Je vous diray: "J'ay tort et honte,
Quoi qu'il m'ait fait, a Dieu remis!"

THE TESTAMENT

At thirty I am not quite sane,
And not quite insane. Finally
I have drunk up all the pain
That Bishop Thibault d'Aussigny
Made me suffer. The man may be
"Bishop of the Streets." That's fine.
The bishop of the whole blessed see,
Provided that he isn't mine.

He isn't bishop over me,
Nor my landlord. It lies fallow.
I do not owe him loyalty,
Am not his serf, and not his doe.
All that I had from him to show
One summer was a loaf of bread.
Stingy or princely? I don't know.
May God feed him as I was fed!

If someone thinks it isn't good
To hear me cursing him this way,
I think he has misunderstood.
I am not cursing. All I say
Is that I hope, on Judgment Day,
By Jesus, King of Paradise,
He will be questioned thoroughly,
As I was, soul and body, twice.

If the man has been more cruel
Than at this time I want to say,
I trust God in his justice will
Put this too in the scales and weigh.
But since the Church says we should pray
For those who hate us, I am leaving
To Him who said, "I will repay,"
The last, eternal reckoning.

Si prieray pour luy de bon cuer,
Et pour l'ame de feu Cotart!
Mais quoy? ce sera donc par cuer,
Car de lire je suis fetart.
Priere en feray de Picart;
S'il ne la scet, voise l'aprendre,
S'il m'en croit, ains qu'il soit plus tart,
A Douai ou a l'Isle en Flandre!

Combien, se oyr veult qu'on prie
Pour luy, foy que doy mon baptesme!
Obstant qu'a chascun ne le crye,
Il ne fauldra pas a son esme.
Ou Psaultier prens, quant suis a mesme,
Qui n'est de beuf ne cordouen,
Le verselet escript septiesme
Du psëaulme *Deus laudem.*

Si prie au benoist fils de Dieu,
Qu'a tous mes besoings je reclame,
Que ma povre priere ait lieu
Vers luy, de qui tiens corps et ame,
Qui m'a preservé de maint blasme
Et franchy de ville puissance.
Loué soit il, et Nostre Dame,
Et Loys, le bon roy de France!

Auquel doint Dieu l'eur de Jacob
Et de Salmon l'onneur et gloire;
Quant de proesse, il en a trop,
De force aussi, par m'ame! voire,
En ce monde cy transitoire,
Tant qu'il a de long et de lé,
Affin que de luy soit memoire,
Vivre autant que Mathusalé!

I'll pray for him with a good heart,
And for the soul of that wide throat
And my close friend, the late Cotart.
But it would only be by rote—
I don't read much although I quote.
I'll say for him a Picard's prayer
From Lille or Douai. He should know it:
They are so piously sincere.

So long as it doesn't get around,
On my baptism I do swear
I'll say one for him I have found
That seems perfect. In the Psalter,
Not bound in cordovan or leather
But plainly. . . at the seventh place
In the "Deus Laudem." Right there,
As though made for the Bishop's case.

 I make my prayer to the One
Who has me always in His care,
My body and my soul, God's Son.
To Him I shall direct my prayer.
He saved me when an evil power
Held me penned in vile durance.
Our Lady too, all praise to her,
And Louis, the good King of France.

God grant him Jacob's happiness,
Solomon's honor and his glory.
He has all he needs of prowess.
In this world that's transitory
He is the happiest king, for he
Shall hear his virtues praised in song
And his deeds extolled in story.
Like Methuselah may he live long!

Et douze beaux enfans, tous masles,
Voire de son chier sang royal,
Aussi preux que fut le grant Charles,
Conceus en ventre nupcial,
Bons comme fut sainct Marcial!
Ainsi en preigne au feu Dauphin!
Je ne luy souhaitte autre mal,
Et puis Paradis en la fin.

Pour ce que foible je me sens
Trop plus de biens que de santé,
Tant que je suis en mon plain sens,
Si peu que Dieu m'en a presté,
Car d'autre ne l'ay emprunté,
J'ay ce testament tres estable
Faict, de derniere voulenté,
Seul pour tout et irrevocable.

Escript l'ay l'an soixante et ung,
Que le bon roy me delivra
De la dure prison de Mehun,
Et que vie me recouvra,
Dont suis, tant que mon cuer vivra,
Tenu vers luy m'humilier,
Ce que feray tant qu'il mourra:
Bienfait ne se doit oublier.

Or est vray qu'après plainz et pleurs
Et angoisseux gemissemens,
Après tristesses et douleurs,
Labeurs et griefz cheminemens,
Travail mes lubres sentemens,
Esguisez comme une pelote.
M'ouvrit plus que tous les Commens
D'Averroys sur Aristote.

And twelve male children may he have,
Born of the royal, wedded house.
Like Charlemagne may they be brave,
And like Saint Martial...pious.
No worse fortune for him and us
I wish than that the King should be
As happy as the Dauphin was,
And Paradise his destiny.

Since it seems I am so poor
In worldly goods, not my body,
And still have all the power
Of such sense as God gave me,
For I borrowed it from nobody,
I have made this my final
Testament, my voluntary
And sole irrevocable will.

Written in fourteen sixty-one
When the King delivered me
From the harsh prison of Mehun
And gave me back my liberty.
Until my dying day I shall be
Filled with heartfelt gratitude
To him, and with humility.
One should not forget the good.

Now after many moans and tears,
Anguished groaning and complaining,
Sadnesses and heavy cares,
Labors and grievous wandering,
My brain, made smooth by studying,
And round and empty as a bottle,
Was more improved by suffering
Than by Averroës on Aristotle.

Combien qu'au plus fort de mes maulx,
En cheminant sans croix ne pille,
Dieu, qui les pelerins d'Esmaus
Conforta, ce dit l'Evangille,
Me monstra une bonne ville
Et pourveut du don d'esperance;
Combien que le pecheur soit ville,
Riens ne hayt que perseverance.

Je suis pecheur, je le sçay bien;
Pourtant ne veult pas Dieu ma mort,
Mais convertisse et vive en bien,
Et tout autre que pechié mort.
Combien qu'en pechié soye mort,
Dieu vit, et sa miséricorde,
Se conscience me remort,
Par sa grace pardon m'accorde.

Et, comme le noble *Rommant*
De la Rose dit et confesse
En son premier commencement
Qu'on doit jeune cuer en jeunesse,
Quant on le voit viel en viellesse,
Excuser, helas! il dit voir;
Ceulx donc qui me font telle presse
En meurté ne me vouldroient veoir.

Se, pour ma mort, le bien publique
D'aucune chose vaulsist mieulx,
A mourir comme ung homme inique
Je me jujasse, ainsi m'aist Dieux!
Griefz ne faiz a jeunes n'a vieulx,
Soie sur piez ou soie en biere:
Les mons ne bougent de leurs lieux,
Pour ung povre, n'avant n'arriere.

In my misfortunes, penniless,
God who spoke so cheeringly
To two on the way to Emmaus
Also showed me a fine city
That held a gift of hope for me.
Sin is vile, but the only one
God won't forgive is obduracy—
Not just sinning but keeping on.

I am a sinner, well I know,
But God does not want me to die.
He wants me to be saved, and so
Others as gnawed with sin as I.
Though deep in sin my life may lie,
God still lives, with his compassion.
If with remorse to Him I cry,
In His grace He will grant pardon.

And as *The Romance of the Rose*
Tells us, what the heart has done
When it was young, one must excuse
When the flower of life is gone
And age, alas! comes creeping on.
Those hunting me would not allow
My life to see another sun,
But would like it to end right now.

If it advanced the public good
To treat me as a criminal,
I would agree, so help me God!
And accept what would befall.
But I have done no harm at all.
Whether on his feet or laid in earth,
The mountains will not rise and fall
For a poor man, or move back and forth.

Ou temps qu'Alixandre regna,
Ung homs nommé Diomedès
Devant luy on luy amena,
Engrillonné poulces et des
Comme ung larron, car il fut des
Escumeurs que voions courir;
Si fut mis devant ce cadès,
Pour estre jugié a mourir.

L'empereur si l'araisonna:
"Pourquoi es tu larron en mer?"
L'autre responce luy donna:
"Pourquoi larron me faiz nommer?
Pour ce qu'on me voit escumer
En une petiote fuste?
Se comme toy me peusse armer,
Comme toy empereur je feusse.

"Mais que veux-tu? De ma fortune,
Contre qui ne puis bonnement,
Qui si faulcement me fortune,
Me vient tout ce gouvernement.
Excuse moy aucunement
Et saiche qu'en grant povreté,
Ce mot se dit communement,
Ne gist pas grande loyauté."

Quant l'empereur ot remiré
De Diomedès tout le dit:
"Ta fortune je te mueray
Mauvaise en bonne," si luy dit.
Si fist il. Onc puis ne mesdit
A personne, mais fut vray homme;
Valere pour vray le baudit,
Qui fut nommé le Grant a Romme.

In the great Alexander's reign
A man by name Diomedes
Was brought before him, with a chain
On each limb, thumbs tied...one of these
Pirates who infest the seas.
And now he was arraigned in court
To be judged for his offences
And have his piracy cut short.

The Emperor asked him, "Why
Do you live by piracy?"
Diomedes answered, "Why
Do you call it piracy?
Only because people see me
Run about in a boat like a shoe.
If I had your arms, believe me,
I'd be an emperor like you.

What do you expect? It was fate.
With fate the bad habits began
That made my life so desperate.
Who can oppose his fate? No man.
Forgive me, Your Honor, if you can,
For know that in great poverty,
As an old saying I've heard ran,
You will not find great loyalty."

The great Alexander pondered
What Diomedes had said,
"I'll change your fate," he thundered
"From bad to good." And he did.
And then Diomedes, who had
A bad habit of cursing too,
Gave it up. This story I read
In Valerius, who says it's true.

Se Dieu m'eust donné rencontrer
Ung autre piteux Alixandre
Qui m'eust fait en bon eur entrer,
Et lors qui m'eust veu condescendre
A mal, estre ars et mis en cendre
Jugié me feusse de ma voix.
Necessité fait gens mesprendre
Et faim saillir le loup du bois.

Je plains le temps de ma jeunesse,
(Ouquel j'ay plus qu'autre gallé
Jusques a l'entree de viellesse),
Qui son partement m'a celé.
Il ne s'en est a pié allé
N'a cheval: helas! comment don?
Soudainement s'en est vollé
Et ne m'a laissié quelque don.

Allé s'en est, et je demeure,
Povre de sens et de savoir,
Triste, failly, plus noir que meure,
Qui n'ay ne cens, rente, n'avoir;
Des miens le mendre, je dis voir,
De me desavouer s'avance,
Oubliant naturel devoir
Par faulte d'ung peu de chevance.

Si ne crains avoir despendu
Par friander ne pas leschier;
Par trop amer n'ay riens vendu
Qu'amis me puissent reprouchier,
Au moins qui leur couste moult chier.
Je le dy et ne croy mesdire;
De ce je me puis revenchier:
Qui n'a mesfait ne le doit dire.

If God had given me the luck
To meet a merciful emperor,
And afterwards I had slid back
Into my sinful ways once more,
I myself would have been all for
Burning me. With my voice I would.
Necessity leads men to error
And brings the wolf out of the wood.

The joyful days of youth are gone.
No one, I think, had more enjoyment
Till age, alas! came creeping on.
My youth vanished in a moment.
Silently stealing, there it went.
Not walking or riding... on the wing
My joyful youth was quickly spent.
It has flown and left me nothing.

I'm still here, though poor in wisdom,
Though with no rent or property
Or any other source of income,
Sad, failing, blacker than a berry.
Even members of my family
Have come forward to denounce me,
Forgetting all their natural duty,
Just because I have no money.

I did not spend it all on eating,
Feasting, or other luxury,
Nor for a woman sold anything
For which friends might reproach me—
At least, that cost them much money.
Of that I can say I'm guiltless.
A man whose conscience is clear and free
As mine has nothing to confess.

Bien est verté que j'ay amé
Et ameroie voulentiers;
Mais triste cuer, ventre affamé
Qui n'est rassasié au tiers,
M'oste des amoureux sentiers.
Au fort, quelqu'ung s'en recompense,
Qui est ramply sur les chantiers;
Car la dance vient de la pance.

Hé! Dieu, se j'eusse estudié
Ou temps de ma jeunesse folle
Et a bonnes meurs dedié,
J'eusse maison et couche molle.
Mais quoi? je fuyoie l'escolle,
Comme fait le mauvais enfant.
En escripvant ceste parolle,
A peu que le cuer ne me fent.

Le dit du Sage trop le feiz
Favorable (bien en puis mais!)
Qui dit: "Esjoys toy, mon filz,
En ton adolescence"; mais
Ailleurs sert bien d'ung autre mes,
Car "Jeunesse et adolescence,"
C'est son parler, ne moins ne mais,
"Ne sont qu'abus et ignorance."

Mes jours s'en sont allez errant
Comme, dit Job, d'une touaille
Font les filetz, quant tisserant
En son poing tient ardente paille:
Lors, s'il y a nul bout qui saille,
Soudainement il le ravit.
Si ne crains plus que rien m'assaille,
Car a la mort tout s'assouvit.

I have loved, and would again,
Gladly. But a heart that's mournful,
And a psyche that never even
Has one third of its belly full,
Have forced me out of the usual
Amorous paths. Give my romance
To someone who doesn't miss a meal.
It's the full belly that makes you dance.

Good God! In my unruly youth
If I'd settled down and studied
And lived virtuously, in truth
I'd have a house and a soft bed.
But they could keep their books! I fled
From school as naughty children do.
Now as I write these words, I shed
Tears, and my heart is breaking too.

"Rejoice in youth," the Prophet writes.
And so I did. In merriment,
Happy days and blissful nights,
My youth, as I have said, was spent.
Then a dish that's very different
He serves you up: to be precise,
All that youth and rejoicing meant,
He says, was ignorance and vice.

The weaver has a straw at hand,
Burning. When a thread hangs down
He touches it quickly with this wand,
And the thread flames and is gone.
My life like that has quickly run,
Job said. And what then should I fear,
Since death soon comes to everyone
And closes out a life of care?

Ou sont les gracieux gallans
Que je suivoye ou temps jadis,
Si bien chantans, si bien parlans,
Si plaisans en faiz et en dis?
Les aucuns sont morts et roidis,
D'eulx n'est il plus riens maintenant:
Repos aient en paradis,
Et Dieu saulve le remenant!

Et les autres sont devenus,
Dieu mercy! grans seigneurs et maistres;
Les autres mendient tous nus
Et pain ne voient qu'aux fenestres;
Les autres sont entrez en cloistres
De Celestins et de Chartreux,
Botez, housez, com pescheurs d'oistres.
Voyez l'estat divers d'entre eux.

Aux grans maistres Dieu doint bien faire,
Vivans en paix et en requoy;
En eulx il n'y a que refaire,
Si s'en fait bon taire tout quoy.
Mais aux povres qui n'ont de quoy,
Comme moy, Dieu doint patience!
Aux autres ne fault qui ne quoy,
Car assez ont pain et pitance.

Bons vins ont, souvent embrochiez,
Saulces, brouetz et gros poissons,
Tartes, flans, oefz fritz et pochiez,
Perdus et en toutes façons.
Pas ne ressemblent les maçons,
Que servir fault a si grant peine:
Ils ne veulent nuls eschançons,
De soy verser chacun se peine.

Where are the fine young men I knew,
Companions in days of old,
Good singers and good talkers too,
Pleasant in their speech and bold?
Some are dead and stiff and cold,
Nothing remains of them today.
May Heaven their restless spirits hold,
And God preserve the ones who stay!

Others have become great men,
Thank God, and masters in the land.
Others may see bread only when
At a window they staring stand.
And some have joined a holy band
Of Celestines or of Chartreux,
In high boots, prayer book in hand.
What different things men have to do!

May God make great men kind.
May they live in peace and quiet.
Nothing will ever change their mind,
So it is better not to try it.
But the poor who are on a diet,
As I am, God grant them patience.
The great need nothing, they're out of sight,
They have their bread and sustenance.

Good wines they have, and often broached,
Sauces, stews, and the bigger fish,
Tarts, custards, eggs fried or poached,
Sugared . . . every kind of dish.
Masons are difficult and bearish.
They want you to wait on them with trays,
To pour their wine, meet every wish.
The poor help themselves, all sorts of ways.

En cest incident me suis mis
Qui de riens ne sert a mon fait;
Je ne suis juge, ne commis
Pour pugnir n'absoudre mesfait:
De tous suis le plus imparfait,
Loué soit le doulx Jhesucrist!
Que par moy leur soit satisfait!
Ce que j'ay escript est escript.

Laissons le moustier ou il est;
Parlons de chose plus plaisante:
Ceste matiere a tous ne plaist,
Ennuyeuse est et desplaisante.
Povreté, chagrine et dolente,
Tousjours despitieuse et rebelle,
Dit quelque parolle cuisante;
S'elle n'ose, si la pense elle.

Povre je suis de ma jeunesse,
De povre et de petite extrace;
Mon pere n'eust oncq grant richesse,
Ne son ayeul, nommé Orace;
Povreté tous nous suit et trace.
Sur les tombeaulx de mes ancestres,
Les ames desquelz Dieu embrasse!
On n'y voit couronnes ne ceptres.

De povreté me garmentant,
Souventesfois me dit le cuer:
"Homme, ne te doulouse tant
Et ne demaine tel douleur,
Se tu n'as tant qu'eust Jaques Cuer:
Mieulx vault vivre soubz gros bureau
Povre, qu'avoir esté seigneur
Et pourrir soubz riche tombeau!"

I'm wandering in a digression
And off the path that I am on.
To punish or forgive transgression
Is not my job. I am not the one
To judge others...the things I've done.
Jesus be praised! May what I say
Help them all to earn a pardon,
And what I have written, let it stay.

Let's leave the church where it is placed
And talk of some more pleasant thing.
This is not to everyone's taste,
It is abrasive and displeasing.
Poverty, grim-visaged, grieving
And insolent, as are the weak,
Always has some word that's cutting,
Or thinks it, if it dare not speak.

Poor I have been, from childhood on,
My people of a humble race.
Great wealth? My father boasted none,
Nor did his grandfather, Horace.
Poverty tracks us. You may trace
On tombs a long line coming down,
Of souls who lie in God's embrace.
No scepters there, and not a crown.

When I grumble of my poverty,
Often my heart speaks to me so:
"Don't give yourself such misery,
And make your grievance such a show.
If you have less than Jacques Coeur, know
It's better to live in coarse clothing
Than to have been a lord and go
And rot in a tomb fit for a king."

Qu'avoir esté seigneur!... Que dis?
Seigneur, las! et ne l'est il mais?
Selon les davitiques dis
Son lieu ne congnoistra jamais.
Quant du surplus, je m'en desmetz:
Il n'appartient a moy, pecheur;
Aux theologiens le remetz,
Car c'est office de prescheur.

Si ne suis, bien le considere,
Filz d'ange portant dyademe
D'estoille ne d'autre sidere,
Mon pere est mort, Dieu en ait l'ame!
Quant est du corps, il gist soubz lame.
J'entens que ma mere mourra,
Et le scet bien, la povre femme,
Et le filz pas ne demourra.

Je congois que povres et riches,
Sages et folz, prestres et laiz,
Nobles, villains, larges et chiches,
Petiz et grans, et beaulx et laiz,
Dames a rebrassez colletz,
De quelconque condicion,
Portans atours et bourreletz,
Mort saisit sans excepcion.

Et meure Paris ou Helaine,
Quiconques meurt, meurt a douleur
Telle qu'il pert vent et alaine;
Son fiel se creve sur son cuer,
Puis sue, Dieu scet quelle sueur!
Et n'est qui de ses maux l'alege:
Car enfant n'a, frere ne seur,
Qui lors voulsist estre son plege.

This was a great lord you said?
Alas, not what he was before?
According to the psalms of David
His place shall know him no more.
Whatever else may lie in store
Is not this sinner's task to tell.
It is the theologian's chore
To know, the preacher's to raise hell.

I do not happen to be the son
Of an angel, as I surely know.
I don't wear a constellation
Of stars above me in a halo.
My father is dead, and lies below,
May God keep his soul! My mother,
The poor woman, will soon follow,
And her son too, soon after her.

As I see it, the fat and lean,
Wise and foolish, priests and lay,
Nobles, peasants, generous, mean,
Great and small, beautiful, ugly,
The with-her-collar-turned-up lady,
Every possible condition
In life, and the fashion industry,
Death seizes—all, with no exception.

Whether it's Paris, or Helen's death,
Whoever dies, dies in great pain.
He can hardly draw a breath,
His heart pressed by a bursting spleen,
And, God, what a sweat he's in!
No one can relieve his agony.
No one, not his closest kin,
Would take his place if that could be.

La mort le fait fremir, pallir,
Le nez courber, les vaines tendre,
Le col enfler, la chair mollir,
Joinctes et nerfs croistre et estendre.
Corps femenin, qui tant es tendre,
Poly, souef, si precieux,
Te fauldra il ces maux attendre?
Oy, ou tout vif aller es cieulx.

BALLADE
Des Dames du Temps Jadis

Dictes moy ou, n'en quel pays,
Est Flora la belle Rommaine,
Archipiada ne Thaïs
Qui fut sa cousine germaine,
Echo parlant quant bruyt on maine
Dessus riviere ou sus estan,
Qui beaulté ot trop plus qu'humaine.
Mais ou sont les neiges d'antan?

Ou est la tres sage Helloïs
Pour qui chastré fut et puis moyne
Pierre Esbaillart a Saint Denis?
Pour son amour ot ceste essoyne.
Semblablement, ou est la royne
Qui commanda que Buridan
Fust geté en ung sac en Saine?
Mais ou sont les neiges d'antan?

La royne Blanche comme lis
Qui chantoit a voix de seraine,
Berte au grant pié, Bietris, Alis,
Haremburgis qui tint le Maine,

He trembles and his face grows pale,
His nose is hooked, his veins distend,
The joints stiffen and they swell
So that the limbs can hardly bend.
Oh female body, soft and tender,
Must you change? Unless mirrors lie,
Even beauty must have an end or,
Still dressing, go up to the sky.

BALLADE
Women of Time Past

Tell me in what country is
Flora the beautiful Roman,
Archipiada, or Thais.
Echo who speaks to no man
Unless he speaks first, then she can
Over a river, lake, or bay,
Was too beautiful to be human.
But where are the snows of yesterday?

Where is the learned Heloise,
For whom was gelded that poor man,
Pierre Abelard of Saint Denis?
With love of her his pains began.
The queen who wanted Buridan
Bagged and dropped in the Seine, they say,
Was a very passionate woman,
But where are the snows of yesterday?

Queen Blanche of the fleur-de-lis,
Who sang so well the people ran...
To hear; Bertha Bigfoot, Alice,
Arembourg, the countess of Maine,

Et Jehanne la bonne Lorraine
Qu'Englois brulerent a Rouan;
Ou sont ilz, ou, Vierge souvraine?
Mais ou sont les neiges d'antan?

Prince, n'enquerez de sepmaine
Ou elles sont, ne de cest an,
Qu'a ce reffrain ne vous remaine:
Mais ou sont les neiges d'antan?

AUTRE BALLADE
Des Seigneurs du Temps Jadis

Qui plus, ou est le tiers Calixte,
Dernier decedé de ce nom,
Qui quatre ans tint le papaliste?
Alphonce le roy d'Aragon,
Le gracieux duc de Bourbon,
Et Artus le duc de Bretagne,
Et Charles septiesme le bon?
Mais ou est le preux Charlemaigne?

Semblablement, le roy Scotiste
Qui demy face ot, ce dit on,
Vermeille comme une amatiste
Depuis le front jusqu'au menton?
Le roy de Chippre de renon,
Helas! et le bon roy d'Espaigne
Duquel je ne sçay pas le nom?
Mais ou est le preux Charlemagne?

D'en plus parler je me desiste;
Le monde n'est qu'abusion.
Il n'est qui contre mort resiste
Ne qui treuve provision.

And Joan the bonny of Lorraine,
Burned by the English... Where are they,
Tell me, O Virgin Sovereign!
But where are the snows of yesterday?

Prince, do not enquire again
Where all those women are today.
All you will hear is the refrain,
But where are the snows of yesterday?

ANOTHER BALLADE
Great Men of Time Past

And more: where is the third Calixtus,
Of his line the most recent one?
Pope for four years, I think he was.
Alfonso, the King of Aragon,
And the gracious Duke of Bourbon?
Brittany's Arthur? I ask in vain.
And Charles the Seventh, a paragon...
But where, O where, is Charlemagne?

Where is the Scottish king, the skin
Of whose face seemed painted, on
One side only, down to his chin,
A brilliant vermilion?
And Cyprus, there's another one...
Also the famous king of Spain
Whose name escapes me... he too's gone.
But where, O where, is Charlemagne?

But I shall speak no more of this—
The world is only a delusion.
To strive against man's dying is
Futile, or to make provision.

Encor fais une question:
Lancelot le roy de Behaigne,
Ou est-il? Ou est son tayon?
Mais ou est le preux Charlemagne?

Ou est Claquin le bon Breton?
Ou le conte Daulphin d'Auvergne
Et le bon feu duc d'Alençon?
Mais ou est le preux Charlemagne

AUTRE BALLADE
En Vieil Langage Françoys

Car, ou soit ly sains apostolles,
D'aubes vestus, d'amys coeffez,
Qui ne saint fors saintes estolles
Dont par le col prent ly mauffez
De mal talant tout eschauffez,
Aussi bien meurt que cilz servans,
De ceste vie cy bouffez:
Autant en emporte ly vens.

Voire, ou soit de Constantinoboles
L'emperieres au poing dorez,
Ou de France ly roy tres nobles
Sur tous autres roys decorez,
Qui pour ly grans Dieux aourez
Bastist eglises et couvens,
S'en son temps il fut honnorez,
Autant en emporte ly vens.

Ou soit de Vienne et de Grenobles
Ly Dauphin, ly preux, ly senez,
Ou de Dijon, Salins et Doles,
Ly sires et ly filz ainsnez,

But I still have one more question:
Ladislaus of Bohemia... Again,
Where have he and his grandfather gone?
But where, O where, is Charlemagne?

Where is Guesclin, the brave Breton?
Does the Dauphin of Auvergne remain,
Or the good Duke of Alençon?
But where, O where, is Charlemagne?

ANOTHER BALLADE
In Old French

Where is the Pope, His Holiness?
Wearing the alb, stole, and amice,
The proper and befitting dress
Of universal love and peace.
In this, his only armor, he's
Fighting the Devil, till the day
He shall have saved from sinfulness
As much as the wind will take away.

Yes, and where's Constantinople's
Golden-fisted emperor?
And, above all other nobles,
He who built another church or
Another convent... praise and honor
To him! And let us also pray
The King of France is sainted for
As much as the wind will take away.

Whether Dauphin of Grenoble,
Vienna, hero of Dijon
Or Salins, senator of Dole,
Heir apparent or oldest son,

Ou autant de leurs gens privez,
Heraulx, trompetes, poursuivans,
Ont ilz bien bouté soubz le nez?
Autant en emporte ly vens.

Princes a mort sont destinez,
Et tous autres qui sont vivans;
S'ilz en sont courciez n'ataynez,
Autant en emporte ly vens.

Puis que papes, roys, filz de roys
Et conceus en ventres de roynes,
Sont ensevelis mors et frois,
En autruy mains passent leurs regnes,
Moy, povre mercerot de Renes,
Mourray je pas? Oy, se Dieu plaist;
Mais que j'aye fait mes estrenes,
Honneste mort ne me desplaist.

Ce monde n'est perpetuel
Quoy que pense riche pillart:
Tous sommes soubz mortel coutel.
Ce confort prens, povre viellart,
Lequel d'estre plaisant raillart
Ot le bruit, lors que jeune estoit,
Qu'on tendroit a fal et paillart,
Se, viel, a railler se mettoit.

Or luy convient il mendier,
Car a ce force le contraint.
Regrete huy sa mort et hier;
Tristesse son cuer si estraint,
Se, souvent, n'estoit Dieu qu'il craint,
Il feroit ung orrible fait;
Et advient qu'en ce Dieu enfraint
Et que luy mesmes se desfait.

And their followers, one by one,
Heralds, trumpets, wouldn't you say
They filled their bellies, and have won
As much as the wind will take away?

Princes must die. It's destiny.
Though it angers them to hear it, they
Have gained by their nobility
As much as the wind will take away.

Since every pope, king, and king's son
Who for his mother had a queen
Will one day be dead and gone,
And to another leave his reign,
I am not going to complain,
A humble peddler. And since I
Have had some fun, and will again—
I don't much mind having to die.

This world is not perpetual
As malefactors seem to hold:
We're under a knife blade, one and all.
Take comfort in this, now you're old:
When you were young you often told
A joke that set the table roaring.
If you tried it now, they'd fold
Their napkins. You'd be very boring.

So now he begs. Necessity
Compels. There is no other way
To stay alive that he can see,
And yet he longs for death each day.
But for the fear of God he may
Do something horrible, commit
An act... driven to disobey
By his suffering, seek to end it.

Car s'en jeunesse il fut plaisant,
Ores plus riens ne dit qui plaise.
Toujours viel cinge est desplaisant,
Moue ne fait qui ne desplaise;
S'il se taist, affin qu'il complaise,
Il est tenu pour fol recreu;
S'il parle, on luy dit qu'il se taise
Et qu'en son prunier n'a pas creu.

Aussi ces povres fameletes
Qui vielles sont et n'ont de quoy,
Quant ilz voient ces pucelletes
Emprunter elles a requoy,
Ils demandent a Dieu pourquoy
Si tost naquirent, n'a quel droit.
Nostre Seigneur se taist tout quoy,
Car au tancer il le perdroit.

La Vieille en Regrettant le Temps
De sa Jeunesse ou les Regrets
De la Belle Heaulmière

Advis m'est que j'oy regreter
La belle qui fut hëaulmiere,
Soy jeune fille soushaitter
Et parler en telle maniere:
"Ha! viellesse felonne et fiere,
Pourquoi m'as si tost abatue?
Qui me tient, qui, que ne me fiere,
Et qu'a ce coup je ne me tue?

"Tollu m'as la haulte franchise
Que beaulté m'avoit ordonné
Sur clers, marchans et gens d'Eglise:
Car lors il n'estoit homme né

They used to think his humor pleasant—
Nothing he says now seems to please.
Old monkeys always are repellent.
If he's silent they say that he's
Senile...it's the old folk's disease.
But if he tries to get in a word,
He's quickly told to hold his peace,
That what he's saying is absurd.

Also, those little old women
Now all alone and penniless,
When they see a sly young virgin
Sneaking in to take their place...
Would the Lord inform them, please,
Why they were born so long ago?
Who made the law? He holds His peace—
He'd lose the argument, you know.

The Old Woman Regretting
The Time of Her Youth, or Lament
Of the Beautiful Helmet Maker

I thought I heard an old woman,
The beautiful Helmet Maker,
Grieving for her youth that's gone,
Speaking of it in this manner:
"Ha! Felonious age, destroyer,
Why did you beat me down this way?
What's to keep me suffering further,
From ending it with a stroke today?

The power I held over men
You took, my beauty at its height.
Clerks, leading merchants, clergymen,
Would have given all for a night

Qui tout le sien ne m'eust donné,
Quoy qu'il en fust des repentailles,
Mais que luy eusse habandonné
Ce que reffusent truandailles.

"A maint homme l'ay reffusé,
Qui n'estoit a moy grant sagesse,
Pour l'amour d'ung garson rusé,
Auquel j'en feiz grande largesse.
A qui que je feisse finesse,
Par m'ame, je l'amoye bien!
Or ne me faisoit que rudesse,
Et ne m'amoit que pour le mien.

"Si ne me sceut tant detrayner,
Fouler aux piez, que ne l'aymasse,
Et m'eust il fait les rains trayner,
S'il m'eust dit que je le baisasse,
Que tous mes maulx je n'oubliasse.
Le gluton, de mal entechié,
M'embrassoit... J'en suis bien plus grasse!
Que m'en reste il? Honte et pechié.

"Or il est mort, passé trente ans,
Et je remains vielle, chenue.
Quant je pense, lasse! au bon temps,
Quelle fus, quelle devenue;
Quant me regarde toute nue,
Et je me voy si tres changiee,
Povre, seiche, megre, menue,
Je suis presque toute enragiee.

"Qu'est devenu ce front poly,
Cheveulx blons, ces sourcils voultiz,
Grant entroeil, ce regart joly,
Dont prenoie les plus soubtilz;

With such beauty, though they might
Regret it later. And would today
If they saw me as I am, a sight
To make a beggar turn away.

Many a man I would refuse—
It wasn't quite so bright of me—
For a smart boy whom I chose,
Fed well, and dressed in finery.
I cheated on him but, believe me,
I loved him, though he drove me mad.
He knocked me around a bit roughly,
And loved me only for what I had.

He could drag me through the mud,
Tread on me ... I loved him more.
Had he maimed me, I still would.
When he told me to kiss him, the sore
Ribs and curses went out the door.
The glutton, full of wickedness,
Embraced me. What did that leave for
Me now? Just shame and sinfulness.

It's thirty years that he's been dead,
And I remain with my gray hair.
When I think of the times I had,
And what I am now! When I stare
At my naked body, and compare
Its dried up, shriveled ugliness
With what it used to be, I swear
I'm filled with such great bitterness!

Where has the smooth forehead gone,
Blond hair, arched eyebrows, wide-spaced eyes,
The playful look that nets the pigeon
However timorous he is, or wise

Ce beaiu nez droit grant ne petiz,
Ces petites joinctes oreilles,
Menton fourchu, cler vis traictiz,
Et ces belles levres vermeilles?

"Ces gentes espaulles menues,
Ces bras longs et les mains traictisses,
Petiz tetins, hanches charnues,
Eslevees propres, faictisses
A tenir amoureuses lisses;
Ces larges rains, ce sadinet
Assis sur grosses fermes cuisses,
Dedens son petit jardinet?

"Le front ridé, les cheveux gris,
Les sourcilz cheus, les yeulx estains,
Qui faisoient regars et ris
Dont mains marchans furent attains;
Nez courbes de beaulté loingtains,
Oreilles pendantes, moussues,
Le vis pally, mort et destains,
Menton froncé, levres peaussues:

"C'est d'umaine beaulté l'issue!
Les bras cours et les mains contraites,
Les espaulles toutes bossues;
Mamelles, quoy? toutes retraites;
Telles les hanches que les tetes;
Du sadinet, fy! Quant des cuisses,
Cuisses ne sont plus, mais cuisettes
Grivelees comme saulcisses.

"Ainsi le bon temps regretons
Entre nous, povres vielles sotes
Assises bas, a crouppetons,
Tout en ung tas comme pelotes,

He thinks he is? To itemize:
A straight nose, neither big nor small,
The ears too, just the perfect size,
And crimson lips, to cap it all.

Pretty shoulders, long and slender
Arms; beautiful hands and wrists,
That my fate seemed to intend for
Heated tourneys in the lists
Of passion... small, tilting breasts,
Rounded thighs, wide loins, and then
The vulva in its little nest
In the middle of the garden.

Wrinkled forehead and gray hair,
Sunken eyebrows, and the eyes
Whose laughter drove men to despair,
Clouding... again to itemize.
The nose that was a perfect size,
Hooked. Two hairy ears hang down.
You'd have to look hard to realize
This death's-head is a face you've known.

The end of beauty isn't good:
Shoulders pulled into a hump,
Arms short, fingers stiff as wood.
The breasts? Shrunk, scarcely a bump.
The same goes for the hips and rump.
The vulva? Ugh! The rounded thigh is
A thigh no more, a shriveled stump
Covered with spots, like sausages.

So now here on our heels we squat,
Each miserable poor old fool,
Talking among ourselves of what
We had, when life was wonderful.

A petit feu de chenevotes
Tost allumees, tost estaintes;
Et jadis fusmes si mignotes!…
Ainsi en prent a mains et maintes."

BALLADE
La Belle Heaulmière
Aux Filles de Joie

"Or y pensez, belle Gantiere
Qui m'escoliere souliez estre,
Et vous, Blanche la Savetiere,
Or est il temps de vous congnoistre.
Prenez a destre et a senestre;
N'espargnez homme, je vous prie:
Can vielles n'ont ne cours ne estre,
Ne que monnoye qu'on descrie.

"Et vous, la gente Saulciciere
Qui de dancier estre adestre,
Guillemete la Tapiciere,
Ne mesprenez vers vostre maistre:
Tost vous fauldra clorre fenestre;
Quant deviendrez vielle, flestrie,
Plus ne servirez qu'ung viel prestre,
Ne que monnoye qu'on descrie.

"Jehanneton la Chapperonniere,
Gardez qu'amy ne vous empestre;
Et Katherine la Bourciere,
N'envoyez plus les hommes paistre:
Car qui belle n'est, ne perpetre
Leur male grace, mais leur rie.
Laide viellesse amour n'empestre,
Ne que monnoye qu'on descrie.

Women are like balls of wool
Close to a fire. Soon set aflame,
And soon burned out. All beautiful
Women like us would say the same."

BALLADE
The Beautiful Helmet Maker
To the Daughters of Joy

"Beautiful Glove Girl, consider.
Blanche the Shoemaker, black or tan,
It's time to think what the future
Holds for both of you. Spare no man!
Grab all the money that you can,
To right and left. Now! Don't wait!
Old women have no more value than
A coin that doesn't circulate.

Sausage Seller, graceful dancer,
And Guillemette for Tapestry,
Don't give your boss a back answer.
Without the shop where'll you be?
With some old priest. All you'll see
For wages—and he'll hate to pay it,
The Lord's work should be done for free—
A coin that doesn't circulate.

You, Bonnet Maker, bonny Jean,
Don't let your boy friend pin you down.
Don't be so choosy, Catherine.
If you want a man all of your own,
Try smiling for a change, don't frown.
A plain girl can always get a date,
But what'll you be when youth has flown?
A coin that doesn't circulate.

"Filles, vueillez vous enremettre
D'escouter pourquoy pleure et crie:
Pour ce que je ne me puis mettre,
Ne que monnoye qu'on descrie."

C'este leçon icy leur baille
La belle et bonne de jadis;
Bien dit ou mal, vaille que vaille,
Enregistrer j'ay faict ces dis
Par mon clerc Fremin l'estourdis,
Aussi rassis que je puis estre.
S'il me desment, je le mauldis:
Selon le clerc est deu le maistre.

Si aperçoy le grant dangier
Ouquel homme amoureux se boute...
Et qui me vouldroit laidangier
De ce mot, en disant: "Escoute!
Se d'amer t'estrange et reboute
Le barat de celles nommees,
Tu fais une bien folle doubte,
Car ce sont femmes diffamees.

"S'ilz n'ayment fors que pour l'argent,
On ne les ayme que pour l'eure;
Rondement ayment toute gent,
Et rient lors que bource pleure.
De celles cy n'est qui ne queure;
Mais en femmes d'onneur et nom
Franc homme, se Dieu me sequeure,
Se doit emploier; ailleurs, non."

Je prens qu'aucun dye cecy,
Si ne me contente il en rien.
En effect il conclut ainsy,
Et je le cuide entendre bien,

Girls, be warned! The reason why
I weep and cry at such a rate,
Is that I'll be like this till I die,
A coin that doesn't circulate."

This was the lesson that she taught
Who once was beautiful and good,
And there it is, well said or not.
I've dictated as well as I could
To Fremin. I hope he understood
And the fool doesn't spoil my work.
He may—his head is made of wood.
People judge the master by the clerk.

So, I see, lives may be wrecked,
That there is danger in such love.
But now someone will object:
"Stop right there," he says. "Enough!
What you're describing isn't love.
All those tricks that women play...
It's loose women you're speaking of,
Hell raisers, and there's hell to pay.

It's money that they love, for sure,
And they take it from anyone.
Their love affairs last an hour.
When purses cry they laugh. Not one
Of the women you name doesn't run
Around. An honest man should know
Women with a good reputation,
So help me, God! Otherwise, no."

I think of someone saying this,
And I don't like it, not a bit.
In effect, his conclusion is,
If I may briefly paraphrase it:

Qu'on doit amer en lieu de bien:
Assavoir mon se ces filletes
Qu'en parolles toute jour tien
Ne furent ilz femmes honnestes?

Honnestes si furent vraiement,
Sans avoir reproches ne blasmes.
Si est vray qu'au commencement
Une chascune de ces femmes
Lors prindrent, ains qu'eussent diffames,
L'une ung clerc, ung lay, l'autre ung moine,
Pour estaindre d'amours les flammes
Plus chauldes que feu saint Antoine.

Or firent selon le Decret
Leurs amys, et bien y appert;
Ilz amoient en lieu secret,
Car autre d'eulx n'y avoit part.
Toutesfois, ceste amour se part:
Car celle qui n'en amoit qu'un
D'iceluy s'eslonge et despart,
Et aime mieulx amer chascun.

Qui les meut a ce? J'ymagine,
Sans l'onneur des dames blasmer,
Que c'est nature femenine
Qui tout vivement veult amer.
Autre chose n'y sçay rimer,
Fors qu'on dit a Rains et a Troys,
Voire a l'Isle et a Saint Omer,
Que six ouvriers font plus que trois.

Or ont ces folz amans le bont
Et les dames prins la vollee;
C'est le droit loyer qu'amans ont:
Toute foy y est viollee,

Love should find a better target.
But I talk to three of these women,
And each of them, if she says it
Herself, had a fine reputation.

They were honest at the start
Deserving no reproach or blame.
Then each chose with all her heart,
And so began their ill fame,
But they were honest all the same.
One chose a layman, one a clerk,
And one a monk, to put out the flame
Of love. It was hot but honest work.

In accord with the Decree
Each had chosen with her heart.
They met their lovers secretly,
Each had her own man, apart.
Then—I don't know how such things start—
Each of them, now she'd begun,
Went and upset the apple cart,
Wanting to love three men, not one.

Why do they do it? I imagine—
I'm not blaming women here—
It's something very feminine:
Love is so nice, they want to share.
Honestly, I have no idea.
As they say at Saint-Denis,
And at Lille and Saint-Omer,
"Six men can do more work than three."

And now the ladies have the ball,
Volley their lovers off the court.
That is the fate, it seems, of all
Game-players of the losing sort.

Quelque doulx baisier n'acollee.
"De chiens, d'oyseaulx, d'armes, d'amours,"
Chascun le dit a la vollee,
"Pour ung plaisir mille doulours."

DOUBLE BALLADE
Sur le Même Propos

Pour ce, amez tant que vouldrez,
Suyvez assemblees et festes,
En la fin ja mieulx n'en vauldrez
Et si n'y romprez que vos testes;
Folles amours font les gens bestes:
Salmon en ydolatria,
Samson en perdit ses lunetes.
Bien est eureux qui riens n'ya a!

Orphëus, le doux menestrier,
Jouant de fleustes et musetes,
En fut en dangier d'un murtrier
Chien Cerberus a quatre testes;
Et Narcisus, le bel honnestes,
En ung parfont puis se noya
Pour l'amour de ses amouretes.
Bien est eureux qui riens n'y a!

Sardana, le preux chevalier,
Qui conquist le regne de Cretes
En voulut devenir moullier
Et filler entre pucelletes;
David le roy, sage prophetes,
Crainte de Dieu en oublia,
Voyant laver cuisses bien faites.
Bien est eureux qui rien n'y a!

Hugs and kisses are sweet but short.
Everyone who plays complains:
With hounds, hawks, arms, and amorous sport,
"For one pleasure, a thousand pains."

DOUBLE BALLADE
On the Same Theme

And so, love to your heart's content,
Go to a party or a feast,
You'll have nothing for all you spent,
And have a broken head at least.
Love turns man into a beast.
Think of blind Samson, of Solomon
With idols as his wives increased.
It's a lucky lover who has none.

The famous flute and bagpipe player
And master singer, Orpheus,
For a wife put his life in danger
Of the dog with four heads, Cerberus.
And the handsome boy, Narcissus,
Whose girls were always coming on,
In a pond sought his quietus.
It's a lucky lover who has none.

Sardanapulus, the man
Who so bravely conquered Crete.
Wanted to become a woman
And sit spinning at their feet.
King David left the judgment seat
And his God, to go spying on
A pair of thighs that were a treat.
It's a lucky lover who has none.

Amnon en voult deshonnourer,
Faignant de menger tarteletes,
Sa seur Thamar et desflourer,
Qui fut inceste deshonnestes;
Herodes, pas ne sont sornetes,
Saint Jehan Baptiste en decola
Pour dances, saulx et chansonnetes.
Bien est eureux qui riens n'y a!

De moy, povre, je vueil parler:
J'en fus batu comme a ru telles,
Tout nu, ja ne le quier celer.
Qui me feist maschier ces groselles,
Fors Katherine de Vausselles?
Noel le tiers ot, qui fut la,
Mitaines a ces nopces telles.
Bien est eureux qui riens n'ya a!

Mais que ce jeune bacheler
Laissast ces jeunes bacheletes?
Non! et le deust on vif brusler
Comme ung chevaucheur d'escouvetes,
Plus doulces luy sont que civetes;
Mais toutesfoys fol s'y fya:
Soient blanches, soient brunetes,
Bien est eureux qui riens n'ya a!

Se celle que jadis servoie
De si bon cuer et loyaument,
Dont tant de maulx et griefz j'avoie
Et souffroie tant de torment,
Se dit m'eust, au commencement,
Sa voulenté (mais nennil, las!),
J'eusse mis paine aucunement
De moy retraire de ses las.

Amnon was in love with his sister
And used sickness as a ruse.
When she brought him cakes he raped her,
Adding incest to abuse.
King Herod felt he couldn't refuse
The ballet dancer who wanted John
The Baptist's head for some strange use.
It's a lucky lover who has none.

Now of myself... To all and sundry,
I have a pleasant tale to tell.
Once I was laid flat like laundry
And beaten. By whose order, tell?
Who but Katherine de Vausselles!
Noel caught it too. While this went on
The wedding guests laughed like hell.
It's a lucky lover who has none.

But that this young bachelor
Give up these young girls in bloom?
Not if he were set on fire
Like the man who rides a broom.
They're sweeter to him than perfume.
Blonde or brunette, whichever one
You see across a crowded room,
It's a lucky lover who has none.

If she whom I served formerly
With such a good and faithful heart,
Who brought such ill and grief to me,
Had let me know right from the start
What she wanted... But she was smart.
Alas, I might have torn the net
She threw around my foolish heart,
But when I knew it was too late.

Quoy que je luy voulsisse dire,
Elle estoit preste d'escouter
Sans m'acorder ne contredire;
Qui plus, me souffroit acouter
Joignant d' elle, pres m'accouter,
Et ainsi m'aloit amusant,
Et me souffroit tout raconter;
Mais ce n'estoit qu'en m'abusant.

Abusé m'a et fait entendre
Tousjours d'ung que ce fust ung aultre,
De farine que ce fust cendre,
D'ung mortier ung chappeau de faultre,
De viel machefer que fust peaultre,
D'ambesars que ce fussent ternes,
(Tousjours trompeur autruy enjaultre
Et rent vecies pour lanternes),

Du ciel une poille d'airain,
Des nues une peau de veau,
Du matin qu'estoit le serain,
D'ung trongnon de chou ung naveau,
D'orde cervoise vin nouveau,
D'une truie ung molin a vent
Et d'une hart ung escheveau,
D'ung gras abbé ung poursuyvant.

Ainsi m'ont Amours abusé
Et pourmené de l'uys au pesle.
Je croy qu'homme n'est si rusé,
Fust fin comme argent de coepelle,
Qui n'y laissast linge, drappelle,
Mais qu'il fust ainsi manyé
Comme moy, qui partout m'appelle
L'amant remys et regnyé.

Whenever I would talk to her
She didn't agree or disagree,
But seemed willingly to hear.
And, what's more, she would let me
Come close and whisper. And so she
Strung me along, led by the nose,
Telling her everything... to be
Made a fool of later, as she chose.

For she could give my head a spin.
Flour was ashes, a bit of iron
Not what I thought it was, but tin.
The bit of cloth the judge put on
When ordering an execution
Was just a hat. These cheats and liars
Know how to foster a delusion,
Take your lanterns and leave you bladders.

The sky is a copper frying pan.
Clouds are really calfskin. Come on!
Do you really think the day began
When you got up? It was going down.
Cabbages are turnips. It's well known,
The fat abbot's in the Bishop's pay.
I hear the hangman's back in town.
You're drinking too much, by the way.

Then love made me turn around,
Pushed me out, and locked the door.
I don't think any man could be found,
Even with brains of silver ore,
Who wouldn't have lost his shirt, or
Worse, if he had been worked over
As I was. People have a name for
Me now: the "I'm against it" lover.

Je regnie Amours et despite
Et deffie a feu et a sang.
Mort par elle me precipite,
Et ne leur en chault pas d'ung blanc.
Ma vielle ay mys soubz le banc;
Amans je ne suyvray jamais:
Se jadis je fus de leur ranc,
Je desclare que n'en suis mais.

Car j'ay mys le plumail au vent,
Or le suyve qui a attente.
De ce me tais doresnavant,
Car poursuivre vueil mon entente.
Et s'aucun m'interroge ou tente
Comment d'Amours j'ose mesdire,
Ceste parolle le contente:
"Qui meurt, a ses loix de tout dire."

Je congnois approcher ma seuf;
Je crache, blanc comme coton,
Jacoppins gros comme ung esteuf.
Qu'est ce a dire? que Jehanneton
Plus ne me tient pour valeton,
Mais pour ung viel usé roquart:
De viel porte voix et le ton,
Et ne suys qu'ung jeune coquart.

Dieu mercy et Tacque Thibault,
Qui tant d'eaue froide m'a fait boire,
Mis en bas lieu, non pas en hault,
Mengier d'angoisse mainte poire,
Enferré...Quant j'en memoire,
Je prie pour luy *et reliqua*,
Que Dieu luy doint, et voire, voire!
Ce que je pense... *et cetera*.

True! I'm against love. I despise it,
Defy it in fire and in blood.
I can pick up my fiddle by the exit
As I leave. She wishes I would.
I can go straight to hell. Understood?
What, they ask, am I waiting for?
All right, I'm going. This time for good.
I won't be coming back any more.

So the wind can have my feather,
And all lovers go with the wind.
I'm out of the game altogether—
If anybody is inclined
To interrogate me, to find
The reason I rail as I do
At love: "A man may speak his mind
When he's dying." Let this content you.

I get an alert when thirst calls
And I spit as white as cotton,
"Jacobins" like tennis balls.
What's there to say? Jehanneton
No longer thinks I'm twenty-one,
But legendary, like the roc,
With an old man's voice and tone,
And yet I'm a young fighting cock.

God be thanked, and Tacque Thilbaut
Who gave me so much cold water,
And not upstairs, but down below,
And made me eat the bitter pear,
In chains. When I remember
I pray for him *et reliqua*:
Dear God, please let him hear
What I think, *et cetera*.

Toutesfois, je n'y pense mal
Pour luys, ne pour son lieutenant,
Aussi pour son official,
Qui est plaisant et advenant;
Que faire n'ay du remenant,
Mais du petit maistre Robert.
Je les ayme, tout d'ung tenant,
Aini que fait Dieu le Lombart.

Si me souvient bien, Dieu mercis,
Que je feis a mon partement
Certains laiz, l'an cinquante six,
Qu'aucuns, sans mon consentement,
Voulurent nommer *Testament;*
Leur plaisir fut et non le mien.
Mais quoi? on dit communement
Qu'ung chascun n'est maistre du sien.

Pour les revoquer ne le dis,
Et y courust toute ma terre;
De pitié je suis refroidis
Envers le Bastart de la Barre:
Parmi ses trois gluyons de fuerre
Je luys donne mes vielles nates;
Bonnes seront pour tenir serre,
Et soy soustenir sur les pates.

S'ainsi estoit qu'aucun n'eust pas
Receu les laiz que je luy mande,
J'ordonne qu'après mon trespas
A mes hoirs en face demande.
Mais qui sont ils? S'on le demande:
Moreau, Provins, Robin Turgis.
De moy, dictes que je leur mande,
Ont eu jusqu'au lit ou je gis.

And yet I don't wish him ill,
Nor his prosecutor, nor
His judge who, for an official,
Is pleasant enough. As for
The others, I'll say nothing more,
With just one little exception,
Master Robert. As Lombards adore
Their God, they all have my devotion.

I remember—and I praise
God for that—before I went
In fifty-six, I made some lays
I thought of as an experiment.
Some people called them my *Testament*.
This wasn't my idea. It was
Circulated without my consent.
Nobody owns what he thinks he does.

But I don't disown my legacies,
Not were all my land at stake.
Tell the Bastard the straw is his,
And three old mats, for old times' sake.
He can pile them up to make
A mattress for his customers
And himself, so his knees won't shake
And slide when he's riding on all fours.

If someone did not receive
His legacy, it's in arrears.
I order that when I leave
Finally, he ask my heirs
To give him that which is not theirs.
But who are they? Provins, Moreau,
Robin Turgis, will have had their shares,
Even my bed. I have willed it so.

Somme, plus ne diray qu'ung mot,
Car commencer vueil a tester:
Devant mon clerc Fremin qui m'ot,
S'il ne dort, je vueil protester
Que n'entens homme detester
En ceste presente ordonnance,
Et ne la vueil magnifester
Si non ou royaume de France.

Je sens mon cuer qui s'affoiblit
Et plus je ne puis papier.
Fremin, sié toy pres de mon lit,
Que l'on ne me viengne espier;
Prens ancre tost, plume et papier;
Ce que nomme escry vistement,
Puys fay le partout coppier;
Et vecy le commancement.

Ou nom de Dieu, Pere eternel,
Et du Filz que vierge parit,
Dieu au Pere coeternel,
Ensemble et le Saint Esperit,
Qui sauva ce qu'Adam perit
Et du pery pare les cieulx...
Qui bien ce croit, peu ne merit,
Gens mors estre faiz petiz dieux.

Mors estoient, et corps et ames,
En dampnee perdicion,
Corps pourris et ames en flammes,
De quelconque condicion.
Toutesfois, fais excepcion
Des patriarches et prophetes;
Car, selon ma concepcion,
Oncques n'eurent grant chault aux fesses.

Now I'll not say another thing,
For I must set about my will
With my clerk who's listening,
If not asleep. I'll say no evil
Of anyone in this present bill
Of legacies, except by chance,
And do not want it published. Still,
I suppose that it could be, in France.

I feel my heart is growing weak
And that the end is drawing near.
Fremin, sit close, so when I speak
No prowling spy will overhear.
Bring your ink and pen and paper,
Quickly. Write what I dictate,
Have copies made, not too dear,
And see to it they circulate.

In the name of God, Father eternal,
And, of virgin born, the Son,
God with the Father coeternal,
And Holy Ghost, the Three in One
Who saved all that was undone
By Adam, and bedecks the skies
With the dead . . . To think they pass on
As little gods merits no mean prize.

They were dead, bodies and souls,
And condemned to perdition,
Bodies rotten, and burning coals
For the spirits . . . everyone,
Always, with the exception
Of the patriarchs and prophets;
For, according to my conception,
None feels much heat where he sits.

Qui me diroit: "Qui vous fait metre
Si tres avant ceste parolle,
Qui n'estes en theologie maistre?
A vous est presumpcion folle."
C'est de Jhesus la parabolle
Touchant du Riche ensevely
En feu, non pas en couche molle,
Et du Ladre de dessus ly.

Se du Ladre eust veu le doit ardre,
Ja n'en eust requis refrigere,
N'au bout d'icelluy doit aherdre
Pour rafreschir sa maschouëre.
Pyons y feront mate chiere,
Qui boyvent pourpoint et chemise,
Puis que boiture y est si chiere.
Dieu nous en gart, bourde jus mise!

Ou nom de Dieu, comme j'ay dit,
Et de sa glorieuse Mere,
Sans pechié soit parfait ce dit
Par moy, plus megre que chimere;
Se je n'ay eu fievre eufumere,
Ce m'a fait divine clemence;
Mais d'autre dueil et perte amere
Je me tais, et ainsi commence.

Premier, je donne ma povre ame
A la benoiste Trinité
Et la commande a Nostre Dame,
Chambre de la divinité
Priant toute la charité
Des dignes neuf Ordres des cieulx
Que par eulx soit ce don porté
Devant le Trosne precieux.

If someone says, "What authority
Gives you the right to lecture us?
What do you know of theology?"
I would remind them of what Jesus
Said. It wasn't a soft mattress
The rich man had, but a bed of fire
In the next world, while Lazarus
The leper got to sit up higher.

If the rich man had seen fire drip
From the leper's finger, he would not
Have wanted even the slightest sip
To cool the burning in his throat.
And drinkers who have always got
A burning thirst, and sell everything
To cool it, will find the water hot
In the place where they are going.

In the Lord's name, as I have said,
And His Mother, may my work be
Guiltless of sin, and perfected—
Finished, that is, if not perfectly.
I didn't have fever, Heaven's mercy
Be thanked! So I shall say no more
About grief and pain and misery,
But start with the items you've waited for.

First: my soul, though it is poor,
I give to the blessed Trinity
And Our Lady who rules over
The chamber of divinity,
And pray for all the charity
Of the nine new orders of the sky,
That this gift they will place for me
Before the precious Throne on high.

Item, mon corps j'ordonne et laisse
A nostre grant mere la terre;
Les vers n'y trouveront grant gresse,
Trop luy a fait fain dure guerre.
Or luy soit delivré grant erre:
De terre vint, en terre tourne;
Toute chose, se par trop n'erre,
Voulentiers en son lieu retourne.

Item, et a mon plus que pere,
Maistre Guillaume de Villon,
Qui esté m'a plus doulx que mere
A enfant levé de maillon:
Degeté m'a de maint bouillon,
Et de cestuy pas ne s'esjoye,
Si luy requier a genouillon
Qu'il m'en laisse toute la joye;

Je luy donne ma librairie,
Et le *Rommant du Pet au Deable,*
Lequel maistre Guy Tabarie
Grossa, qui est homs veritable.
Par cayers est soubz une table;
Combien qu'il soit rudement fait,
La matiere est si tres notable
Qu'elle amende tout le mesfait.

Item, donne a ma povre mere
Pour saluer nostre Maistresse,
(Qui pour moy ot douleur amere,
Dieu le scet, et mainte tristesse):
Autre chastel n'ay, ne fortresse,
Ou me retraye corps et ame,
Quant sur moy court malle destresse,
Ne ma mere, la povre femme!

Item: my body I donate
To the mother of us all, the earth;
The worms won't find much fat on it
For hunger has reduced its girth.
Let her have it for what it's worth,
And soon. From dust it goes to dust.
"Wherefore then hast thou brought me forth?"
Everything goes back, as it must.

Item: to my more than father,
Master Guillaume de Villon,
Who has been gentler than a mother
With a misbehaving little son...
He got me out of scrapes, and this one
Isn't making him happy. On my knees
I implore him not to take this on.
Let me have all the joy of it, please!

I bequeath him my library
And *Romance of the Farting Devil,*
Which Master Guy Tabarie
Copied, and keeps under the table.
I took some notes when I was able.
I can't commend the rough-hewn style,
But the subject is...notable,
And makes the time you spend worthwhile.

Item: I caused my poor mother
A great deal of unhappiness
At one time and another.
I have neither castle nor fortress
To leave her, only this address.
No sure refuge but Our Lady
In times of danger or distress
Did I ever have, nor will she.

BALLADE
Pour Prier Nostre Dame

Dame du ciel, regente terrienne,
Emperiere des infernaux palus,
Recevez moy, vostre humble chrestienne,
Que comprinse soye entre vos esleus,
Ce non obstant qu'oncques rien ne valus.
Les biens de vous, ma Dame et ma Maistresse,
Sont trop plus grans que ne suis pecheresse,
Sans lesquelz biens ame ne peut merir
N'avoir les cieulx. J n'en suis jangleresse:
En ceste foy je vueil vivre et mourir.

A vostre Filz dictes que je suis sienne;
De luy soyent mes pechiez abolus;
Pardonne moy comme a l'Egipcienne,
Ou comme il feist au clerc Theophilus,
Lequel par vous fut quitte et absolus,
Combien qu'il eust au deable fait promesse.
Preservez moy de faire jamais ce,
Vierge portant, sans rompure encourir,
Le sacrement qu'on celebre a la messe:
En ceste foy je vueil vivre et mourir.

Femme, je suis povrette et ancienne,
Qui riens ne sçay; oncques lettre ne lus.
Au moustier voy dont suis paroissienne
Paradis paint, ou sont harpes et lus,
Et ung enfer ou dampnez sont boullus:
L'ung me fait paour, l'autre joye et liesse.
La joie avoir me fay, haulte Deesse,
A qui pecheurs doivent tout recourir,
Comblez de foy, sans fainte ne paresse.
En ceste foy je vueil vivre et mourir.

BALLADE
A Prayer to Our Lady

Lady in Heaven, Empress here on earth
Of swamps and other infernal places,
Though I am a woman of little worth,
Receive me, a Christian, on my knees,
As one of the elect. Your kindnesses
And bounty, dear Mistress, far outweigh
My sins, and so, humbly to you I pray.
Without your kindness poor souls such as I
Cannot go to heaven. There is no way.
In this faith I desire to live and die.

Say to your Son that I am all his own.
By Him may my sins be all wiped away.
May He forgive my sins as once was done
With the Egyptian. Theophilus, they say,
His sins too were absolved, wiped clean away,
Although he was promised to the Devil.
Save me from doing anything so evil!
O woman without sin, who bear on high
The sacrament, I am not worthy. Still,
In this faith I desire to live and die.

I am a poor woman and very old.
I cannot read and I know nothing.
At the church I belong to, I behold
Heaven painted, harps and lutes are playing,
And a Hell where the damned are boiling.
Heaven gives me joy, Hell great distress.
Let me have the joy, heavenly Goddess
To whose mercy all sinners must apply,
Filled with their faith, not faintheartedness.
In this faith I desire to live and die.

V *ous portastes, digne Vierge, princesse,*
I *esus regnant qui n'a ne fin ne cesse.*
L *e Tout Puissant, prenant nostre foiblesse,*
L *aissa les cieulx et nous vint secourir,*
O *ffrit a mort sa tres chiere jeunesse;*
N *ostre Seigneur tel est, tel le confesse.*
En ceste foy je vueil vivre et mourir.

Item, m'amour, ma chiere rose,
Ne luy laisse ne cuer ne foye;
Elle ameroit mieulx autre chose,
Combien qu'elle ait assez monnoye.
Quoy? une grant bource de soye,
Plaine d'escuz, parfonde et large;
Mais pendu soit il, que je soye,
Qui luy laira escu ne targe.

Car elle en a, sans moy, assez.
Mais de cela il ne m'en chault;
Mes plus grans dueilz en sont passez,
Plus n'en ay le croppion chault.
Si m'en desmetz aux hoirs Michault,
Qui fut nommé le Bon Fouterre;
Priez pour luy, faictes ung sault:
A Saint Satur gist, soubz Sancerre.

Ce non obstant, pour m'acquitter
Envers Amours, plus qu'envers elle,
Car oncques n'y peuz acquester
D'espoir une seule estincelle
(Je ne sçay s'a tous si rebelle
A esté, ce m'est grant esmoy;
Mais, par sainte Marie la belle!
Je n'y voy que rire pour moy),

V *irgin Mother, you gave to us, princess,*
I *esu your son whose kingdom is endless,*
L *eaving his power to take on our weakness,*
L *eaving heaven to help such as am I,*
O *ffering death his young manliness.*
N *o other Lord have we, let us confess.*
In this faith I desire to live and die.

Item: to my love, my dear rose,
I leave neither my heart nor faith.
She would like better, I suppose,
Something else I could bequeath.
What? Let's say a silk purse with
A lot of coins. Let it be
Full and deep and large underneath,
But hang the man who gives her money!

She has enough, she doesn't need mine.
It doesn't bother me to know,
For my worst troubles in that line
Are past. The fire is out below.
I leave it to the heirs of Michault,
The Mighty Fucker. Say a prayer
For him, with a somersault or two.
He's at Saint Satur, beneath Sancerre.

Nevertheless, to pay a debt
I owe some women, if not her,
(For never once could I get
A spark out of her. If she were
As cold to others, I'm not sure.
This question used to bother me,
But whichever, a teaser or pure,
The not so funny joke's on me),

Ceste ballade luy envoye
Qui se termine tout par R.
Qui luy portera? Que je voye.
Ce sera Pernet de la Barre,
Pourveu, s'il rencontre en son erre
Ma damoiselle au nez tortu,
Il luy dira, sans plus enquerre:
"Orde paillarde, dont viens tu?"

BALLADE
A s'amye

F *aulse beauté qui tant me couste chier,*
R *ude en effect, ypocrite doulceur,*
A *mour dure plus que fer a maschier,*
N *ommer que puis, de ma desfaçon seur,*
C *herme felon, la mort d'ung povre cuer,*
O *rgueil mussié qui gens met au mourir,*
Y *eulx sans pitié, ne veult Droit de Rigueur,*
S *ans empirer, ung povre secourir?*

M *ieulx m'eust valu avoir esté serchier*
A *illeurs secours: c'eust esté mon onneur;*
R *iens ne m'eust sceu lors de ce fait hachier.*
T *rotter m'en fault en fuyte et deshonneur.*
H *aro, haro, le grant et le mineur!*
E *t qu'est ce cy? Mourray sans coup ferir?*
Ou Pitié veult, selon ceste teneur,
Sans empirer, ung povre secourir?

Ung temps viendra qui fera dessechier,
Jaunir, flestrir vostre espanye fleur;
Je m'en risse, se tant peusse maschier
Lors; mais nennil, ce seroit donc foleur:

I send this ballade that rhymes on R
To Lady Twisted Nose. Who'll take it?
I think friend Pernet with the Bar,
On one condition. When they meet
He'll say, without missing a beat,
Not one word less or one word more,
Right in the middle of the street,
"Where have you been, you dirty whore?"

BALLADE
To His Girlfriend

F *alse beauty who has cost me so dear,*
R *epulsive beneath a mask that is fair,*
A *love that is hard to chew as leather,*
N *ame that I'm sure is ruin's harbinger,*
C *harm of a poor heart the destroyer,*
O *f many this secret pride the slayer,*
Y *es, without pity. Will Justice not hear,*
S *aving a poor man who is in despair?*

M *ore luck I'd have had as a traveler*
A *nd seeker of help. I'd have had honor,*
R *id of this passion's enthralling power.*
T *ake refuge I must in flight and dishonor.*
H *elp! Help! I call and there is no answer,*
E *cho is all. Shall I fall in silence, or*
Words I have spoken will Pity not hear,
Saving a poor man who is in despair?

A season is coming that will wither,
Yellow, shrivel your full-blown flower.
I would laugh to see it, but then I fear
My lungs would no longer have the vigor.

Viel je seray; vous, laide, sans couleur;
Or beuvez fort, tant que ru peut courir;
Ne donnez pas a tous ceste douleur,
Sans empirer, ung povre secourir.

Prince amoureux, des amans le greigneur,
Vostre mal gré ne vouldroye encourir,
Mais tout franc cuer doit pour Nostre Seigneur,
Sans empirer, ung povre secourir.

Item, a maistre Ythier Marchant,
Auquel mon branc laissai jadis,
Donne, mais qu'il le mette en chant,
Ce lay contenant des vers dix,
Et, au luz, ung *De profundis*
Pour ses anciennes amours
Desquelles le nom je ne dis,
Car il me haroit a tous jours.

LAY
Ou Rondeau

Mort, j'appelle de ta rigueur,
Qui m'as ma maistresse ravie,
Et n'es pas encore assouvie
Se tu ne me tiens en langueur:
Onc puis n'eus force ne vigueur;
Mais que te nuysoit elle en vie,
              Mort?

Deux estions et n'avions qu'ung cuer;
S'il est mort, force est que devie,
Voire, ou que je vive sans vie
Comme les images, par cuer,
              Mort!

I would be old, you ugly, with no color.
So drink deeply while the rivers still pour.
Do not give others this grievous dolor,
Saving a poor man who is in despair.

Amorous Prince, the greatest lover,
Your ill will I would not like to bear,
But every kind heart should follow Our Master
Saving a poor man who is in despair.

Item: Master Ythier Marchant
I left my sword. Here is a lay
In ten lines that he may want
To make a love song of, a *De*
Profundis. It's really not a lay
But a rondeau. I haven't said
Her name and given him away.
He'd never forgive me if I did.

LAY
Or Rondeau

Death, I appeal your harsh decree
That has taken my love away.
Still you follow me night and day.
You want something more from me,
For I have no strength or energy.
What harm did she ever do you, say,
        Death?

We were two but we had one heart.
As it is dead I cannot stay,
Or I would have to live as may
Images, without a heart.
        Death!

Item, a maistre Jehan Cornu
Autre nouveau laiz lui vueil faire,
Car il m'a tous jours secouru
A mon grant besoing et affaire;
Pour ce, le jardin luy transfere,
Que maistre Pierre Bobignon
M'arenta, en faisant refaire
L'uys et redrecier le pignon.

Par faulte d'ung uys, j'y perdis
Ung grez et ung manche de houe.
Alors huit faulcons, non pas dix,
N'y eussent pas prins une aloue.
L'ostel est seur, mais qu'on le cloue.
Pour enseigne y mis ung havet;
Qui que l'ait prins, point ne m'en loue:
Sanglante nuyt et bas chevet!

Item, et pour ce que la femme
De maistre Pierre Saint Amant
(Combien, se coulpe y a a l'ame,
Dieu luy pardonne doulcement!)
Me mist ou renc de cayement,
Pour le Cheval Blanc qui ne bouge
Luy chanjay a une jument,
Et la Mulle a ung asne rouge.

Item, donne a sire Denis
Hesselin, esleu de Paris,
Quatorze muys de vin d'Aulnis
Prins sur Turgis a mes perilz.
S'il en buvoit tant que peris
En fust son sens et sa raison,
Qu'on mette de l'eaue es barilz:
Vin pert mainte bonne maison.

Item: to Master Jehan Cornu
I gave a lay. Here's a new one,
For he always helped me through
My troubles. He can have the garden
That Master Pierre Bobignon
Rented me. The missing door
Has to be repaired and put back on,
The gable raised. There's nothing more.

Thanks to the door, somebody got
A hoe handle and a paving stone.
Ten falcons couldn't have caught
A lark in there. It was wide open.
The house is pretty safe, but when
I hung a hook up as a sign,
Someone hooked it. I wish him seven
Bloody nights on a hard bed, the swine.

Item: and because the wife
Of Master Pierre Saint Amant
(If her soul with sin is rife,
May God pardon her, I can't)
Put me down as an "indigent,"
For *The White Horse* that stands still
I'm giving a mare that's different,
And red ass for *The She-Mule* as well.

Item: I give to Sire Denis
Hesselin, duty and excise free,
Fourteen barrels of wine from Aulnis
Taken from Turgis and charged to me.
If he should drink so much that he
Doesn't make sense as he boozes,
Fill all the barrels instantly
With water. Wine has sunk good houses.

Item, donne a mon advocat,
Maistre Guillaume Charruau,
(Quoy que Marchant l'ot par estat)
Mon branc; je me tais du fourreau.
Il aura avec ung rëau
En change, affin que sa bource enfle,
Prins sur la chaussee et carreau
De la grant cousture du Temple.

Item, mon procureur Fournier
Aura pour toutes ses corvees
(Simple sera de l'espargnier)
En ma bource quatre havees,
Car maintes causes m'a sauvees,
Justes, ainsi Jhesu Christ m'aide!
Comme telles se sont trouvees;
Mais bon droit a bon mestier d'aide.

Item, je donne a maistre Jacques
Raguier *le Grant Godet* de Greve,
Pourveu qu'il paiera quatre plaques,
(Deust il vendre, quoy qu'il luy griefve,
Ce dont on cueuvre mol et greve,
Aller sans chausses, en eschappin),
Se sans moy boit, assiet ne lieve,
Au trou de *la Pomme de Pin.*

Item, quant est de Merebeuf
Et de Nicolas de Louviers,
Vache ne leur donne ne beuf,
Car vachiers ne sont ne bouviers,
Mais gens a porter espreviers,
Ne cuidez pas que je me joue,
Et pour prendre perdris, plouviers,
Sans faillir, sur la Machecoue.

Give my sword to my attorney
Master Guillaume Charruau.
He has some complaint about his fee.
(I gave it to Marchant—he needn't know.)
With the sword he'll also have a *rëau*
To make the purse feel more ample
He picked up walking Lawyers' Row
In the inner court of the Temple.

Item: my advocate Fournier
For such outstanding legal service,
(*It would be simple not to pay*),
Four handfuls out of my purse.
He has won me many a case...
All honestly, I understand,
And I don't ask. I could do worse
When justice needs a helping hand.

Item: I bequeath *The Great Wine Cup*
Of Greve to Master Jacques
Raguier. But he must cough up,
As an entrance fee, four plaques
(Even sell the clothes off his back,
Thigh and calf), with this exception:
He can have a drink with me, and crack
Nuts at the famous *Pine Cone Tavern.*

Item: I leave to Merebeuf
And Nicolas de Louviers,
Neither bull nor cow, hide nor hoof.
They have no knack at all that way.
Now—I mean every word I say—
I'm not joking. Let them try
Widow Machecou's. They may
Learn from her how to herd poultry.

Item, viengne Robin Turgis
A moy, je luy paieray so vin;
Combien, s'il treuve mon logis,
Plus fort sera que le devin.
Le droit luy donne d'eschevin,
Que j'ay comme enfant de Paris:
Se je parle ung peu poictevin,
Ice m'ont deux dames apris.

Elles sont tres belles et gentes,
Demourans a Saint Generou
Pres Saint Julien de Voventes,
Marche de Bretaigne ou Poictou.
Mais i ne di proprement ou
Yquelles passent tous les jours;
M'arme! i ne seu mie si fou,
Car i vueil celer mes amours.
Item, a Jehan Raguier je donne,
Qui est sergent, voire des Douze,
Tant qu'il vivra, ainsi l'ordonne,
Tous les jours une tallemouse,
Pour bouter et fourrer sa mouse,
Prinse a la table de Bailly;
A Maubué sa gorge arrouse,
Car au mengier n'a pas failly.

Item, et au Prince des Sotz
Pour ung bon sot Michault du Four,
Qui a la fois dit de bons mots
Et chante bien "Ma doulce amour!"
Je lui donne avec le bonjour;
Brief, mais qu'il fust ung peu en point,
Il est ung droit sot de sejour,
Et est plaisant ou il n'est point.

Item: send Robin Turgis
To me. I'll pay him what I owe
For the wine. The only trouble is,
If he finds out where I live, he's so
Suspicious...I think I'll go
And say I'll make him a magistrate...
That I was born in Paris, you know,
Which gives me the right to confer it.

Yes, I'm from Paris. The slight accent
I picked up at Saint Generou
Near Saint Julien de Voventes.
They're beautiful and nice girls too.
But that's enough. I'm not telling you
Where any day they can be found.
I'm not one of the idiots who
Pass their girlfriends' names around.
Item: for Sergeant Jehan Raguier,
I will that he be taken daily
For a cheese tart or cheese soufflé
Right in the snout, along with Bailly.
Then, for the drink he loves so dearly,
Over to the fountain at Maubué.
That should fill his stomach fairly
And kill his appetite for the day.

To the Prince of Fools, good morning!
I have one for you, Michault du Four.
He can be witty, and likes to sing
"My Sweet Love." Though his jokes are poor,
When he tells one he's such a bore
He's funny. It doesn't make sense.
You could appoint him Professor
Of Foolishness in Residence.

Item, aux Unze Vingtz Sergens
Donne, car leur fait est honneste
Et sont bonnes et doulces gens,
Denis Richier et Jehan Valette,
A chascun une grant cornete
Pour pendre a leurs chappeaulx de faultres;
J'entens a ceulx a pié, hohete!
Car je n'ay que faire des autres.

De rechief donne a Perrenet,
J'entens le Bastart de la Barre,
Pour ce qu'il est beau filz et net,
En son escu, en lieu de barre,
Trois dez plombez, de bonne carre,
Et ung beau joly jeu de cartes.
Mais quoy? s'on l'oyt vecir ne poirre,
En oultre aura les fievres quartes.

Item, ne vueil plus que Cholet
Dolle, trenche, douve ne boise,
Relie broc ne tonnelet,
Mais tous ses houstilz changier voise
A une espee lyonnoise,
Et retienge le hutinet;
Combien qu'il n'ayme bruyt ne noise,
Si luy plaist il ung tantinet.

Item, je donne a Jehan le Lou,
Homme de bien et bon marchant,
Pour ce qu'il est linget et flou,
Et que Cholet est mal serchant,
Ung beau petit chiennet couchant
Qui ne laira poullaille en voye,
Ung long tabart et bien cachant
Pour les mussier, qu'on ne les voye.

Item: I give to Paris's Finest,
Kind and gentle too I bet,
Because their calling is so honest,
Denis Richier and Jehan Vallette,
To each a big strip of velvet
On their felt hat so it hangs down.
I mean the ones on foot. Let's get
Cracking! The horses I disown.

And now I'm back to Perrenet,
I mean the Bastard with a Bar.
Because he's so...what shall I say?
Acceptable...replace the bar.
It really looks too sinister.
Have instead three loaded dice
And a pack of cards. If you should hear
Him fart, give him a fever, twice.

Item: I don't want Cholet
Banging, twisting hoops of iron,
And sawing staves. Throw his tools away,
And give him a sword, a quiet one,
The kind they're making in Lyons.
But keep the mallet. It could come in
Handy later. He's not so down on
A bit of a racket now and then.

Item: I give to Jehan le Lou,
A man of standing and good merchant,
But thin enough to be seen through,
And Cholet's no good at the hunt,
A fine little hound that can point
And doesn't let chickens pass him by,
And very long cloak, so they won't
Be seen by a suspicious eye.

Item, a l'Orfevre de Bois,
Donne cent clouz, queues et testes,
De gingembre sarrazinois,
Non pas pour acouppler ses boetes,
Mais pour conjoindre culz et coetes,
Et couldre jambons et andoulles,
Tant que le lait en monte aux tetes
Et le sang en devalle aux coulles.

Au cappitaine Jehan Riou,
Tant pour luy que pour ses archiers,
Je donne six hures de lou,
Qui n'est pas viande a porchiers,
Prins a gros mastins de bouchiers,
Et cuites en vin de buffet.
Pour mengier de ces morceaulx chiers,
On en feroit bien ung malfait.

C'est viande ung peu plus pesante
Que duvet n'est, plume, ne liege.
Elle est bonne a porter en tente,
Ou pour user en quelque siege.
S'ilz estoient prins a un piege,
Que ces mastins ne sceussent courre,
J'ordonne, moy qui suis son miege,
Que des peaulx, sur l'iver, se fourre.

Item, a Robinet Trascaille,
Qui en service (c'est bien fait)
A pié ne va comme une caille,
Mais sur roncin gras et reffait,
Je lui donne, de mon buffet,
Une jatte qu'emprunter n'ose;
Si aura mesnage parfait:
Plus ne luy failloit autre chose.

Item: to de Bois the Goldsmith,
A hundred ginger cloves—not nails
To put boxes together with,
But Saracen cloves, heads and tails
That will connect males and females,
Hams and sausages, so nipples
Fill up with milk, and whole pails
Of blood run down to the testicles.

Item: to Captain Jehan Riou
Six wolf heads—not just for his men,
The archers, but for him too.
The wolves were tracked down and taken
By big butchers' wolfhounds. Then
Cooked in cheap wine. Dishes like this
Come dear. There are men and women
Who would kill for such delicacies.

It's a bit heavier, this meat,
Than feathers, cork, or eiderdown,
It's good for front line troops to eat,
Or a siege when supplies are down.
If those big dogs couldn't run
And the wolves were caught in traps,
As his doctor I want him to put on,
In winter, wolf fur coats and caps.

Item: to Robinet Trascaille
Who's on the job, and not on foot...
He doesn't go walking like a quail
But rides a horse, well fed and fat.
There is a bowl in my pantry that
He'd like to borrow, but he's shy.
Now he'll be comfy as a cat,
And he should be fixed completely.

Item, donne a Perrot Girart,
Barbier juré du Bourg la Royne,
Deux bacins et ung coquemart,
Puis qu'a gaignier met telle paine.
Des ans y a demie douzaine
Qu'en son hostel de cochon gras
M'apatella une sepmaine,
Tesmoing l'abesse de Pourras.

Item, aux Freres mendians,
Aux Devotes et aux Beguines,
Tant de Paris que d'Orleans,
Tant Turlupins que Turlupines,
De grasses souppes jacoppines
Et flans leur fais oblacion;
Et puis après, soubz ces courtines,
Parler de contemplacion.

Si ne suis je pas qui leur donne,
Mais de tous enffans sont les meres,
Et Dieu, qui ainsi les guerdonne,
Pour qui seuffrent paines ameres.
Il faut qu'ilz vivent, les beaulx peres,
Et mesmement ceulx de Paris.
S'ilz font plaisir a nos commeres,
Ilz ayment ainsi leurs maris.

Quoy que maistre Jehan de Poullieu
En voulsist dire *et reliqua,*
Contraint et en publique lieu,
Honteusement s'en revoqua.
Maistre Jehan de Mehun s'en moqua;
De leur façon si fist Mathieu;
Mais on doit honnorer ce qu'a
Honnoré l'Eglise de Dieu.

Item: to Perrot Girart, who is
Licensed barber at Bourg la Reine,
Two basins and a pot, because
He works so hard. Half a dozen
Years ago, I took shelter in
Girart's house. As God's my witness,
For a week he fed me on bacon.
When you're in Pourras, ask the Abbess.

Item: the Filles Dieu and Beguines,
And other of the Mendicants,
Turlupins and Turlupines,
Either of Paris or Orleans,
Thick, Jacobin stews and flans
I give to them as an oblation.
Afterwards, behind drawn curtains
They may talk of contemplation.

I'm not the one who gives them this,
But every mother of a child,
And God, from Whom every guerdon is,
For all they suffer, meek and mild.
When they live in Paris, domiciled,
As blessed fathers needs must do,
Pleasure our wives and drive them wild,
It's their way of loving husbands too.

Whatever Jehan de Poullieu
Said against them was jumped on.
He would be mortified and made to
Retract in public. Jehan de Mehun
And Matheolus both poked fun
At Mendicants. But we must honor
What the Church says. God's will be done.
It's His Church—I can't turn on her.

Si me soubmectz, leur serviteur
En tout ce que puis faire et dire,
A les honnorer de bon cuer
Et obeïr, sans contredire;
L'homme bien fol est d'en mesdire,
Car, soit a par ou en preschier
Ou ailleurs, il ne fault pas dire
Se gens sont pour eulx revenchier.

Item, je donne a frere Baude,
Demourant en l'ostel des Carmes,
Portant chiere hardie et baude,
Une sallade et deux guysarmes,
Que Detusca et ses gens d'armes
Ne lui riblent sa caige vert.
Viel est: s'il ne se rent aux armes,
C'est bien le deable de Vauvert.

Item, pour ce que le Scelleur
Maint estront de mouche a maschié,
Donne, car homme est de valeur,
Son seau d'avantage crachié,
Et qu'il ait le poulce escachié,
Pour tout empreindre a une voye;
J'entens celuy de l'Eveschié,
Car les autres, Dieu les pourvoye!

Quant des auditeurs messeigneurs,
Leur granche ilz auront lambroissee;
Et ceulx qui ont les culz rongneux,
Chascun une chaire percee;
Mais qu'a la petite Macee
D'Orléans, qui ot ma sainture,
L'amende soit bien hault tauxee:
Elle est une mauvaise ordure.

So I submit, their servitor
In all that I may do and say,
With goodwill to give them honor,
Without contradicting, to obey.
Speak against them, and you'll pay.
They'll be at you from the pulpit,
Or in some hidden, devious way
They'll know how to get even for it.

Item: This is Brother Baude's.
He lives in Carmes, at the hostel.
He's bold and brave. Give him two halberds,
And let him have a sallet as well.
Detusca and his guards won't be able
To break in and rob his green cage.
He's old. He must be Vauvert's devil
If he doesn't ground arms, at his age.

Item: Our Keeper of the Seal
Has had to chew so much bee shit—
And yet he's a worthy man, I feel—
Before you send wax to him, spit
On it. Take his thumb and flatten it,
So when he presses the wax will make
A perfect seal. If he has a fit?
It's the Sealer's job, for Heaven's sake!

The barn of gentlemen auditors
Will have new paneling, complete.
All itching bottoms will have chairs
With access through a hole in the seat.
But that little Macee who looks so sweet
And made off with my belt and purse,
Fine her! And make her wash her feet.
She's a filthy slut—they don't come worse.

Item, donne a maistre Françoys,
Promoteur, de la Vacquerie
Ung hault gorgerin d'Escossoys,
Toutesfois sans orfaverie;
Car, quant receut chevallerie
Il maugrea Dieu et saint George:
Parler n'en oit qui ne s'en rie,
Comme enragié, a plaine gorge.

Item, a maistre Jehan Laurens,
Qui a les povres yeulx si rouges
Pour le pechié de ses parens
Qui burent en barilz et courges,
Je donne l'envers de mes bouges
Pour tous les matins les torchier;
S'il fust arcevesque de Bourges,
Du sendail eust, mais il est chier.

Item, a maistre Jehan Cotart,
Mon procureur en court d'Eglise,
Devoye environ ung patart,
(Car a present bien m'en advise),
Quant chicaner me feist Denise,
Disant que l'avoye mauldite;
Pour son ame, qu'es cieulx soit mise,
Ceste oroison j'ai cy escripte.

BALLADE
Et Oraison

Pere Noé, qui plantastes la vigne,
Vous aussi, Loth, qui beustes ou rochier,
Par tel party qu'Amours, qui gens engigne,
De voz filles si vous feist approuchier
(Pas ne le dy pour le vous reprouchier),

Item: Master Françoys, attorney
Of the Vacquerie...one of those
High Scottish neck bands. Let it be
Without adornment, I like plain clothes.
When he was dubbed a knight, with blows
For God and Saint George, how he swore!
Everyone who's heard of it and knows
The man, laughs like mad, then laughs some more.

Item: to Master Jehan Laurens
Whose eyes are always burning red
Due to the sinning of his parents
Who'll drink from a pail or hogshead,
I give the cover from off my bed
To wipe his eyes with. It should be
Silk, if he were Archbishop instead
Of Bourges, but still too dear for me.

Item: for my lawyer Jehan Cotart
To whom I think I owe a penny
For a case he took in the Church court—
It comes back now: Denise accused me
Of having abused her verbally—
May his soul be transported where
There's always good wine, and it's free...
I have written the following prayer.

BALLADE
And Prayer

Father Noah who first planted the vine;
You also, Lot, who got drunk in the cave,
So that Love, that can turn men into swine,
Made you lie with your daughters (but we don't have
To be judged for sin this side of the grave);

Archetriclin, qui bien sceustes cest art,
Tous trois vous pry qu'o vous vueillez perchier
L'ame du bon feu maistre Jehan Cotart.

Jadis extraict il fut de vostre ligne,
Luy qui buvoit du meilleur et plus chier,
Et ne deust il avoir vaillant ung pigne;
Certes, sur tous, c'estoit ung bon archier;
On ne luy sceut pot des mains arrachier;
De bien boire ne fut oncques fetart.
Nobles seigneurs, ne souffrez empeschier
L'ame du bon feu maistre Jehan Cotart!

Comme homme beu qui chancelle et trepigne
L'ay veu souvent, quant il s'alloit couchier,
Et une fois il se feist une bigne,
Bien m'en souvient, a l'estal d'ung bouchier;
Brief, on n'eust sceu en ce monde serchier
Meilleur pyon, pour boire tost et tart.
Faictes entrer quant vous orrez huchier
L'ame du bon feu maistre Jehan Cotart!

Prince, il n'eust sceu jusqu'a terre crachier;
Tousjours crioit: "Haro! la gorge m'art."
Et si ne sceust oncq sa seuf estanchier
L'ame du bon feu maistre Jehan Cotart.

Item, vueil que le jeune Merle
Desormais gouverne mon change,
Car de changier enys me mesle,
Pourveu que tousjours baille en change,
Soit a privé soit a estrange,
Pour trois escus six brettes targes,
Pour deux angelotz ung grant ange:
Car amans doivent estre larges.

Architriclinus, for the wine-maker's art...
All three, to whom such pleasure wine gave,
Pray for the soul of Master Jehan Cotart.

He could surely have traced his lineage
To one of you, for he drank of the best
Sought after and most expensive vintage,
While at sheer guzzling he beat all the rest.
It was almost impossible to wrest
The jug from his hands when he had a head start.
If you had seen it you'd have been impressed
By the fierce thirst of Master Jehan Cotart.

Like an old man stumbling and stamping his feet,
I often saw him...."A caution," they said.
Once he came staggering down the street
With an enormous bump on his forehead.
I remember it well. Is he really dead?
He took good company so much to heart. . . .
If you hear a knock when you've gone to bed,
Let in the soul of the late Jehan Cotart.

Prince, he couldn't have spat to the ground.
"I'm on fire!" he'd shout. "Where's the water cart?"
Enough wine for his throat could never be found
By the soul of the good late Jehan Cotart.

Item: I want young Merle to run
My exchange business from now on,
For changing money is no fun.
I'm making only this provision:
Let him deal fairly with everyone,
Native or foreign: six Breton *targes*
For three *écus;* two *angelots,* one
Big *ange.* Lovers' purses should be large.

Item, j'ay sceu en ce voyage
Que mes trois povres orphelins
Sont creus et deviennent en aage
Et n'ont pas testes de belins,
Et qu'enfans d'icy a Salins
N'a mieulx sachans leur tout d'escolle.
Or, par l'ordre des Mathelins,
Telle jeunesse n'est pas folle.

Si vueil qu'ilz voisent a l'estude;
Ou? sur maistre Pierre Richier.
Le Donat est pour eulx trop rude:
Ja ne les y vueil empeschier.
Ils sauront, je l'ayme plus cher,
Ave salus, tibi decus,
Sans plus grans lettres enserchier:
Tousjours n'ont pas clers l'au dessus.

Cecy estudient, et ho!
Plus proceder je leurs deffens.
Quant d'entendre le grant *Credo*,
Trop forte elle est pour telz enfans.
Mon long tabart en deux je fens;
Si vueil que la moitié s'en vende
Pour leur en acheter des flans,
Can jeunesse est ung peu friande.

Et vueil qu'ilz soient informez
En meurs, quoy que couste bature;
Chaperons auront enformez
Et les poulces sur la sainture,
Humbles a toute creature,
Disans: "Han? Quoy? Il n'en est rien!"
Si diront gens, par adventure:
"Vecy enfans de lieu de bien!"

Item: while traveling I heard
That my three poor little orphans
Are coming of age and have matured;
That they don't have sheep's brains,
And, in fact, from here to Salins,
No children are so quick in school.
By the Order of the Mathurins
It's clear not one of them's a fool.

So I want them to study. Where?
With Master Pierre Richier.
The *Donat*'s too hard for them, I fear.
Don't put obstacles in their way.
Let them learn—I prefer it anyway—
Ave salus, tibi decus,
Scholars aren't always on top today.
A little learning should do for us.

Going further commonsense forbids.
Let them study that, then whoa!
It's much too hard a task for kids
To understand the great *Credo.*
I'll tear my long coat in two,
And sell half. I know what pleases youth.
The proceeds of the sale may go
To buy them pies for their sweet tooth.

I want them to be trained in good
Manners: when they walk abroad,
To bury their head in their hood,
And be humble—not yell, "Oh Lord!"
When a full chamberpot is poured
Over their head. They'll just call,
"No harm!" People will pass the word:
"They must be the children from the Hall."

Item, et mes povres clerjons,
Auxquels mes tiltres resigné:
Beaulx enfans et droiz comme jons
Les voyant, m'en dessaisiné,
Cens recevoir leur assigné,
Seur comme qui l'auroit en paulme,
A ung certain jour consigné,
Sur l'ostel de Gueuldry Guillaume.

Quoy que jeunes et esbatans
Soient, en riens ne me desplaist:
Dedens trente ans ou quarante ans
Bien autres seront, se Dieu plaist.
Il fait mal qui ne leur complaist;
Ilz sont tres beaulx enfans et gens;
Et qui les bat ne fiert, fol est,
Car enfans si deviennent gens.

Les bources des Dix et Huit Clers
Auront; je m'y vueil travaillier:
Pas ilz ne dorment comme loirs
Qui trois mois sont sans resveillier.
Au fort, triste est le sommeillier
Qui fait aisier jeune en jeunesse
Tant qu'en fin lui faille veillier,
Quant reposer deust en viellesse.

Si en escrips au collateur
Lettres semblables et pareilles:
Or prient pour leur bienfaicteur,
Ou qu'on leur tire les oreilles,
Aucunes gens ont grans merveilles
Que tant m'encline vers ces deux;
Mais, foy que doy festes et veilles,
Oncques ne vy les meres d'eulx!

Item: I have given my titles
To my clerks. Just looking at them
Decided me: though they are little,
As straight as reeds, and so handsome.
They now have an assured income:
The rent, to be paid on a fixed day,
From the house of Gueuldry Guillaume,
Assigned and entered properly.

Though they are young and mischievous,
That really doesn't bother me.
In forty years they'll be like us,
Much changed, perhaps by piety.
One shouldn't treat them cruelly:
They are so gentle. Anyone
Who strikes or beats them has to be
Mad. They'll be people later on.

The pension of a College Clerk
Will be theirs one day, I undertake...
And that they won't sleep at work,
Like dormice. It can really make
You sad, that you're obliged to shake
Them often, or their eyelids close.
Youth should be eager and awake.
Age is the time for such repose.

I'll be writing to the collator,
Letters like this. The little dears
Should pray for me, their benefactor.
If they don't, someone pull their ears!
If my fondness for these two appears
Strange, I assure you, I never
On any occasion met their mothers,
At a feast or fast...whatever.

Item, donne a Michault Cul d'Oue
Et a sire Charlot Taranne
Cent solz (s'ilz demandent: "Prins ou?"
Ne leur chaille; ils vendront de manne)
Et unes houses de basanne,
Autant empeigne que semelle,
Pourveu qu'ilz me salueront Jehanne,
Et autant une autre comme elle.

Item, au seigneur de Grigny,
Auquel jadis laissay Vicestre,
Je donne la tour de Billy
Pourveu, se huys y a ne fenestre
Qui soit ne debout ne en estre,
Qu'il mette tres bien tout a point.
Face argent a destre et senestre:
Il m'en fault et il n'en a point.

Item, a Thibault de la Garde...
Thibault? je mens, il a nom Jehan;
Que luy donray je, que ne perde?
(Assez ay perdu tout cest an;
Dieu y vueille pourveoir, *amen!*)
Le Barillet, par m'ame, voire!
Genevoys est plus ancien
Et a plus beau nez pour y boire.

Item, je donne a Basennier,
Notaire et greffier criminel,
De giroffle plain ung pannier
Prins sur maistre Jehan de Ruel,
Tant a Mautaint, tant a Rosnel,
Et, avec ce don de giroffle,
Servir de cuer gent et ysnel
Le seigneur qui sert saint Cristofle,

Item: give Michault Cul d'Oue
And to Sire Charlot Taranne,
Each of them, a hundred sous.
If they ask, "From where?" Like manna,
Say, from heaven. And you can
Throw in my boot of old leather
If they pay a visit to Jehanne,
And there's another just like her.

I gave Bicêtre formerly
To the Lord of Grigny and his heirs.
He may have the tower of Billy,
Provided that he makes repairs
Of missing doors and windows. There's
The entire roof to be put on.
He'd better have some bright ideas.
I've not much money, and he has none.

To Thibault de la Garde...Why use
That name? His real one is Jehan.
What shall I give that he won't lose?
(I've lost enough since the year began;
May God provide—no other can!)
The Wine Cask? Yes, that's it, I think!
(Genevoys is an older man
And has a finer nose for drink.)

Item: to Basennier,
Notary and criminal
Clerk, a basket of cloves today,
From master Jehan de Ruel—
Some from Mautaint, some Rosnel—
And with this gift of cloves, the prayer
That he may serve with heart and will
The lord who serves Saint Christopher,

Auquel ceste ballade donne
Pour sa dame, qui tous biens a;
S'Amour ainsi tous ne guerdonne,
Je ne m'esbays de cela,
Car au pas conquester l'ala
Que tint Regnier, roy de Cecille,
Ou si bien fist et peu parla
Qu'oncques Hector fist ne Troïlle.

BALLADE
Pour Robert d'Estouteville

A *u poinct du jour, que l'esprevier s'esbat,*
M *eu de plaisir et par noble coustume,*
B *ruit la maulvis et de joye s'esbat,*
R *eçoit son per et se joinct a sa plume,*
O *ffrir vous vueil, a ce desir m'alume,*
I *oyeusement ce qu'aux amans bon semble.*
S *achiez qu'Amour l'escript en son volume;*
E *t c'est la fin pour quoy sommes ensemble.*

D *ame serez de mon cuer sans debat,*
E *ntierement, jusques mort me consume.*
L *orier souef qui pour mon droit combat,*
O *livier franc, m'ostant, toute amertume,*
R *aison ne veult que je desacoustume,*
E *t en ce vueil avec elle m'assemble,*
De vous servir, mais que m'y accoustume;
Et c'est la fin pour quoy sommes ensemble.

Et qui plus est, quant dueil sur moy s'embat,
Par Fortune qui souvent si se fume,
Vostre doulx oeil sa malice rabat,
Ne mais ne mains que le vent fait la plume.
Si ne pers pas la graine que je sume
En vostre champ, quant le fruit me ressemble.
Dieu m'ordonne que le fouysse et fume;
Et c'est la fin pour quoy sommes ensemble.

To whom I offer this ballade
For his lady's grace and beauty.
Very few men does Love reward
Like this. But he won her fairly.
At the tournament in Sicily
Held by Regnier, he was famous:
He fought so well, and modestly,
Like another Hector or Troilus.

BALLADE
For Robert d'Estouteville

A *t dawn when the falcon beats his wings,*
M *oved by pleasure and his noble nature,*
B *lackbirds flutter and the female sings,*
R *eceiving her mate, feather joined to feather,*
O *n fire with my love I wish to offer*
I *n joy what lovers like to dwell upon.*
S *o has Love written and bound in leather:*
E *veryone who's married does. It's the reason.*

D *o not doubt, you are my heart's true bride,*
E *ntirely unto death, come what may.*
L *aurel, to fight bravely at my side*
O *live, to drive all bitterness away.*
R *eason forbids my leaving custom's way,*
(E *ven in this, she and I think as one*)
Drives me to serve you this and every day.
Everyone who's married does. It's the reason.

And what is more, whenever grief comes near,
Brought by Dame Fortune, who is often cursed,
Your gentle glance makes malice disappear
Like smoke by a temperate wind dispersed.
I shall not have lost my labor when the first
Fruit resembles me. So God's will be done,
I delve and plant. Let Fortune do her worst.
Everyone who's married does. It's the reason.

Princesse, oyez ce que cy vous resume:
Que le mien cuer du vostre desassemble
Ja ne sera; tant de vous en presume;
Et c'est la fin pour quoy sommes ensemble.

Item, a sire Jehan Perdrier,
Riens, n'a Françoys, son secont frere.
Si m'ont voulu tous jours aidier,
Et de leurs biens faire confrere;
Combien que Françoys, mon compere,
Langues cuisans, flambans et rouges,
My commandement my priere,
Me recommanda fort a Bourges.

Si allé veoir en Taillevent,
Ou chappitre de fricassure,
Tout au long, derriere et devant,
Lequel n'en parle jus ne sure.
Mais Macquaire, je vous asseure,
A tout le poil cuisant ung deable,
Affin qu'il sentist bon l'arsure,
Ce *recipe* m'escript, sans fable.

BALLADE

En realgar, en arcenic rochier,
En orpiment, en salpestre et chaulx vive,
En plomb boullant pour mieulx les esmorchier,
En suif et poix destrempez de lessive
Faicte d'estrons et de pissat de juifve,
En lavailles de jambes a meseaulx,
En racleure de piez et vels houseaulx,
En sang d'aspic et drogues venimeuses,
En fiel de loups, de regnars et blereaulx,
Soient frittes ces langues envieuses!

Princess, now listen to what I say:
Between my heart and yours division
Will never be if you feel the same way.
Everyone who's married does. It's the reason.

Item: to the two Perdriers,
Jean, and his brother Françoys, nothing!
For they tried to help me always.
Though once, when I was traveling
And the brothers and I were talking,
The younger, Françoys, urged me to try
The red tongue in Bruges. Maybe joking...
I did, and thought that I would die.

So I looked into Taillevent
For what he says on fricassees.
I've looked on every page but can't
Find any items. Lacking these,
Macquaire who, if you please,
Once cooked a devil, with the hair,
Wrote me the following recipes.
The smell...you may get wind of it here.

BALLADE

In arsenic from pulverized rock,
Trisulphide, quicklime, and saltpeter,
In lead boiling to break up the stock,
In soot and pitch and lye that is pure,
Made from a Jewess's feces and her
Urine, also from water used in washing
The legs of lepers, and from the scraping
Of feet, the shed skin of an asp beside,
Wolf, fox, badger's gall . . . in anything,
May those malicious tongues be fried.

En cervelle de chat qui hayt peschier,
Noir, et si viel qu'il n'ait dent en gencive,
D'ung viel mastin, qui vault bien aussi chier,
Tout enragié, en sa bave et salive,
En l'escume d'une mulle poussive
Detrenchiee menu a bons ciseaulx,
En eaue ou ratz plongent groings et museaulx,
Raines, crappaulx et bestes dangereuses,
Serpens, lesars et telz nobles oyseaulx,
Soient frittes ces langues envieuses!

En sublimé, dangereux a touchier,
Et ou nombril d'une couleuvre vive,
En sang qu'on voit es palletes sechier
Sur ces barbiers, quant plaine lune arrive,
Dont l'ung est noir, l'autre plus vert que cive,
En chancre et fiz, et en ces ors cuveaulx
Ou nourrisses essangent leurs drappeaulx,
En petiz baings de filles amoureuses
(Qui ne m'entent n'a suivy les bordeaulx)
Soient frittes ces langues envieuses!

Prince, passez tous ces frians morceaulx,
S'estamine, sacs n'avez, ou bluteaulx,
Parmy le fons d'unes brayes breneuses;
Mais, par avant, en estrons de pourceaulx
Soient frittes ces langues envieuses!

Item, a maistre Andry Courault,
Les Contrediz Franc Gontier mande;
Quant du tirant seant en hault,
A cestuy la riens ne demande.
Le Saige ne veult que contende
Contre puissant povre homme las,
Affin que ses fillez ne tende
Et qu'il ne trebuche en ses las.

In the brains of a cat that hates to fish,
Black, and with no teeth left in its gum,
In the saliva of an old hound which
Is raging with rabies, froth, and scum,
In the foam of a mule beaten like a drum,
Cut up with a scissors in little pieces,
In water in which rats swim with feces,
Frogs, toads, wild animals from far and wide,
Serpents, lizards, everything that pisses,
May those malicious tongues be fried.

In sublimate that poisons with a drop,
In the navel of a snake that's still alive,
In bowls of blood at the barbershop,
Nights when you see a full moon arrive
Half of it black, half greener than chive,
In ulcers, sores, and what's left in the pan
Where nurses rinse diapers if they can,
In the sinks on which amorous girls ride
(If you don't understand, you're a nice man)
May those malicious tongues be fried.

Prince, strain all these good things to eat.
If you don't have a strainer, use the seat
Of an old pair of trousers, deep and wide.
First dip them in pig shit. Then see to it:
May those malicious tongues be fried.

Item: to Master Andry Courault,
I send *Against Franc Gontier.*
As for the tyrant, don't give blow
For blow, but simply turn away,
As the sage says. A poor man may
Not fight with such. He spreads a net,
And the one who's standing in his way
Will stumble and be caught in it.

Gontier ne crains: il n'a nuls hommes
Et mieulx que moy n'est herité;
Mais en ce debat cy nous sommes,
Car il loue sa povreté,
Estre povre yver et esté,
Et a felicité repute
Ce que tiens a maleureté.
Lequel a tort? Or en dispute.

BALLADE
Lez Contrediz de Franc Gontier

Sur mol duvet assis, ung gras chanoine,
Lez ung brasier, en chambre bien natee,
A son costé gisant dame Sidoine,
Blanche, tendre, polie et attintee,
Boire ypocras, a jour et a nuytee,
Rire, jouer, mignonner et baisier,
Et nu a nu, pour mieulx des corps s'aisier,
Les vy tous deux, par ung trou de mortaise:
Lors je congneus que, pour dueil appaisier,
Il n'est tresor que de vivre a son aise.

Se Franc Gontier et sa compaigne Helaine
Eussent ceste doulce vie hantee,
D'oignons, civotz, qui causent forte alaine,
N'acontassent une bise tostee,
Tout leur mathon, ne toute leur potee,
Ne prise ung ail, je le dy sans noysier.
S'ils se vantent couchier soubz le rosier,
Lequel vault mieux? Lict costoyé de chaise?
Qu'en dites vous? Faut il a ce musier?
Il n'est tresor que de vivre a son aise.

De gros pain bis vivent, d'orge, d'avoine,
Et boivent eaue tout au long de l'anee.
Tous les oyseaulx d'icy en Babiloine

Not Gontier...that's not who I meant.
He has no power, no more than I,
But we're embroiled in argument.
The man praises his poverty,
How poor he is, and how nice to be,
Winter and summer, day in, day out,
Whereas it is sheer hell for me.
That's what the argument's about.

BALLADE
Against Franc Gontier

A fat canon, sitting on eiderdown,
A warm stove, thick carpets everywhere,
At his side My Lady Sidoine,
A tender, smooth, white skin, beautiful hair
Done in the latest mode, the happy pair
Laughing, caressing, naked, in broad day,
Drinking and making love...this was the play
I saw through a crack in the wall, on my knees,
And I knew then that to drive grief away
There is no treasure like living at your ease.

If Gontier and his Helaine ever had
A taste of such a sweet, intimate scene,
For onions, scallions, things that make breath bad,
They wouldn't have given...a single bean.
As for their curds and stock pot, I don't mean
To offend, but I don't give a clove. To lie
Under a rose bush? With a couch nearby?
What do you think? Do you agree with these
Who think you should walk furrows till you die?
There is no treasure like living at your ease.

Oat or barley bread, that's what they live on,
And water, only water, every day.
Not all the birds from here to Babylon

A tel escot une seule journee
Ne me tendroient, non une matinee.
Or s'esbate, de par Dieu, Franc Gontier,
Helaine o luy, soubz le bel esglantier:
Se bien leur est, cause n'ay qu'il me poise;
Mais, quoy que soit du laboureux mestier,
Il n'est tresor que de vivre a son aise.

Prince, jugiez, pour tous nous accorder.
Quant est de moy, mais qu'a nul ne desplaise,
Petit enfant, j'ay oy recorder:
Il n'est tresor que de vivre a son aise.

Item, pour ce que scet sa Bible
Ma damoiselle de Bruyeres,
Donne preschier lors l'Evangille
A elle et a ses bachelieres,
Pour retraire ces villotieres
Qui ont le bec si affillé,
Mais que ce soit hors cymetieres,
Trop bien au Marchié au fillé.

BALLADE
Des Femmes de Paris

Quoy qu'on tient belles langagieres
Florentines, Veniciennes,
Assez pour estre messagieres,
Et mesmement les ancïennes;
Mais, soient Lombardes, Rommaines,
Genevoises, a mes perilz,
Pimontoises, Savoisiennes,
Il n'est bon bec que de Paris.

De tres beau parler tiennent chaieres,
Ce dit on, les Neapolitaines,
Et sont tres bonnes caquetieres

Could hold me to that diet. Did I say
Every day? Not even a morning. If they,
Franc Gontier and Helaine, wish to frolic
Under a hawthorn, I don't give a lick.
Though it may be nice to live with birds and bees,
A simple peasant life, with country music,
There is no treasure like living at your ease.

Prince, you judge, and settle this some way.
I hope what I have said does not displease.
When I was a child I heard people say,
There is no treasure like living at your ease.

Item: because she knows her Bible
I grant Mademoiselle de Bruyères
The right to preach, except the Gospel,
Both her and her female followers,
So they can salvage the street walkers
Whose rough tongues rasp like a file.
But not in the graveyard...for such talkers
The Linen Market is more their style.

BALLADE
Of the Women of Paris

Though they're said to be good speakers
Florentine women and Venetian,
Quite good enough for love affairs—
So were the ancient Greek and Roman—
Whether they're Lombard or Romanian,
From Genoa or Piedmontese,
Or women of Savoy, I maintain
There is no tongue like one from Paris.

The art of oratory, I hear,
Is taught at Naples. In Germany
And Prussia, women blithely chatter.

Allemandes et Pruciennes;
Soient Grecques, Egipciennes,
De Hongrie ou d'autre pays,
Espaignolles ou Cathelennes,
Il n'est bon bec que de Paris.

Brettes, Suysses, n'y sçavent guieres,
Gasconnes, n'aussi Toulousaines:
De Petit Pont deux harengieres
Les concluront, et les Lorraines,
Engloises et Calaisiennes,
(Ay je beaucoup de lieux compris?)
Picardes de Valenciennes;
Il n'est bon bec que de Paris.

Prince, aux dames Parisiennes
De beau parler donnez le pris;
Quoy qu'on die d'Italiennes,
Il n'est bon bec que de Paris.

Regarde m'en deux, trois, assises
Sur le bas du ply de leurs robes;
En ces moustiers, en ces eglises;
Tire toy pres, et ne te hobes;
Tu trouveras la que Macrobes
Oncques ne fist tels jugemens.
Entens; quelque chose en desrobes:
Ce sont tous beaulx enseignemens.

Item, et au mont de Montmartre,
Qui est ung lieu moult ancïen,
Je luy donne et adjoings le tertre
Qu'on dit le mont Valerien,
Et, oultre plus, ung quartier d'an
Du pardon qu'apportay de Romme:
Si ira maint bon crestien
Voir l'abbaye ou il n'entre homme.

In Greece and Egypt, in Hungary,
In fact, wherever you may be,
The sound of female voices carries...
In Calais and Chillchester-on-Sea.
But there's no tongue like one from Paris.

Swiss women and English women,
Those of Toulouse or Picardy—
Two Petit Pont fishwomen
Would send the lot off with a flea
In the ear. The same for Gascony.
A Spanish woman when she marries
Takes a vow of silence instantly.
There is no tongue like one from Paris.

Prince, please give the Parisiennes
The prize for talking, for there is,
Whatever may be said of Italians,
After all, no tongue like one from Paris.

Look at them now, in twos and threes,
On the end of a long gown they sit,
Gathered in chapels and in churches.
Draw near them, and be still. Admit,
Macrobius for all his wit
Never made judgments such as these.
You surely have learned something from it:
Such beautiful thoughts, and nice knees.

Item: to Montmartre's mount, to own,
I hereby am bequeathing an
Adjoining piece of land that's known
Locally as Mount Valerien;
Also, a quarter of the pardon
I brought from Rome, that from now on
Many a faithful Christian
May see the abbey where none has gone.

Item, varletz et chamberieres
De bons hostelz (riens ne me nuyt)
Feront tartes, flans et goyeres
Et grant rallias a mynuit
Riens n'y font sept pintes ne huit,
Tant que gisent seigneur et dame:
Puis après, sans mener grant bruit,
Je leur ramentoy le jeu d'asne.

Item, et a filles de bien,
Qui ont peres, meres et antes,
Par m'ame! je ne donne rien,
Car j'ay tout donné aux servantes.
Si fussent ilz de peu contentes:
Grant bien leur fissent mains loppins
Aux povres filles (ennementes!)
Qui se perdent aux Jacoppins,

Aux Celestins et aux Chartreux;
Quoy que vie mainent estroite,
Si ont ilz largement entre eulx
Dont povres filles ont souffrete;
Tesmoing Jaqueline, et Perrete,
Et Ysabeau qui dit: "Enné!";
Puis qu'ilz en ont telle disette,
A paine en seroit on damné.

Item, a la Grosse Margot,
Tres doulce face et pourtraicture,
Foy que doy *brulare bigod,*
Assez devote creature;
Je l'aime de propre nature,
Et elle moy, la douce sade:
Qui la trouvera d'aventure,
Qu'on luy lise ceste ballade.

Item: chambermaids and servants
In big houses (at no cost to me)
Will make everything everyone wants
To eat. At midnight there will be
Tarts, cheese pies, flans, and the drinks are free.
Then, without making a lot of noise—
Not a peep out of my lord and lady—
They'll play the game the ass enjoys.

Item: to girls born into wealth,
Who have fathers, mothers, aunts,
Nothing! I drink to their health,
I gave all I had to the servants.
To make those poor girls content
Would take only a tidbit or two,
But instead it's all being sent
To the Jacobins, that crafty crew,

The Celestines and Carthusians.
They live by strict rules they are set,
But what the famished, suffering ones
Do not receive, the brothers get—
Say Jacqueline and Perrete,
And Ysabeau..."By the Lord, bigod!"
She says. As they are suffering yet,
I hope that He will spare the rod.

Item: as for Fat Margot,
As sweet and pretty as a picture,
She is so stuck on me, so
Devoted, I can't help loving her.
If by chance you're going there,
Would you read her this ballade.
Urgent business calls me elsewhere.
I'd take it kindly. Yes, begad.

BALLADE
De la Grosse Margot

Si j'ayme et sers la belle de bon hait,
M'en devez vous tenir ne vil ne sot?
Elle a en soy des biens a fin souhait.
Pour son amour sains bouclier et passot;
Quant viennent gens, je cours et happe ung pot,
Au vin m'en fuis, sans demener grant bruit;
Je leur tens eaue, frommage, pain et fruit.
S'ilz paient bien, je leur dis: "Bene stat;
Retournez cy, quant vous serez en ruit,
En ce bordeau ou tenons nostre estat!"

Mais adoncques il y a grant deshait,
Quant sans argent s'en vient couchier Margot;
Veoir ne la puis, mon cuer a mort la hait.
Sa robe prens, demy saint et surcot,
Si luy jure qu'il tendra pour l'escot.
Par les costés se prent cest Antecrist,
Crie, et jure par la mort Jhesucrist
Que non fera. Lors j'empoingne ung esclat;
Dessus so nez luy en fais ung escript,
En ce bordeau ou tenons nostre estat.

Puis paix se fait, et me fait ung gros pet,
Plus enflee qu'ung vlimeux escharbot.
Riant, m'assiet son poing sur mon sommet,
Go, go, me dit, et me fiert le jambot.
Tous deux yvres, dormons comme ung sabot.
Et, au resveil, quant le ventre luy bruit,
Monte sur moy, que ne gaste son fruit.
Soubz elle geins, plus qu'un aiz me fait plat;
De paillarder tout elle me destruit,
En ce bordeau ou tenons nostre estat.

BALLADE
Of Fat Margot

If I love and serve the beautiful lady
Do you have to think I'm a vile sot?
She is all a man could want her to be.
For her love with sword and shield I've fought.
When people come I run and get a pot
And fill it with wine on the q. t.
I serve them water, cheese, bread, and fruit.
If they pay well, "Bene stat. You're a sport,"
I say. "When you're in rut again, do it
In this brothel where we are holding court."

But sometimes there's a terrific row,
When Margot comes to bed moneyless.
I can't look at her, I want her dead right now.
I'll take her coat, her sash and her dress
For the fee, I tell her, and for laziness.
With fists on hips, "It's the Antichrist!"
She yells, and swears, by the death of Christ,
I can't do it. I pick up a slat. I ought
To send her a message: she's overpriced
In this brothel where we are holding court.

Then we make peace, and she, inflated
More than a poisonous dung beetle,
Farts. She puts a fist to my forehead.
"Gogo," she says. Then we get drunk until
We fall asleep. When we wake up she'll
Have a rumbling belly. So the fruit won't drop
And be wasted, she says, and climbs on top.
This screwing is cutting my life span short.
I'm groaning underneath, and it doesn't stop
In this brothel where we are holding court.

Vente, gresle, gelle, j'ay mon pain cuit.
Ie suis paillart, la paillarde me duit.
Lequel vault mieulx? Chascun bien s'entresuit.
L'ung vault l'autre; c'est a mau rat mau chat.
Ordure amons, ordure nous assuit;
Nous deffuyons onneur, il nous deffuit,
En ce bordeau ou tenons nostre estat.

Item, a Marion l'Idolle
Et la grant Jehanne de Bretaigne
Donne tenir publique escolle
Ou l'escollier le maistre enseigne.
Lieu n'est ou ce marchié se tiengne,
Si non a la grisle de Mehun;
De quoy je dis: "Fy de l'enseigne,
Puis que l'ouvrage est si commun!"

Item, et a Noel Jolis,
Autre chose je ne luy donne
Fors plain poing d'osiers frez cueillis
En mon jardin; je l'abandonne.
Chastoy est une belle aulmosne,
Ame n'en doit estre marry:
Unze vings coups luy en ordonne
Livrez par la main de Henry.

Item, ne sçay qu'a l'Ostel Dieu
Donner, n'a povres hospitaulx;
Bourdes n'ont icy temps ne lieu,
Car povres gens ont assez maulx.
Chascun leur envoye leurs aulx;
Les Mendians ont eu mon oye;
Au fort, ilz en auront les os:
A menue gent menue monnoye.

Item, je donne à mon barbier,
Qui se nomme Colin Galerne,
Pres voisin d'Angelot l'erbier,

Come wind, hail, or frost, this life is mine.
I'm rotten, this rotten woman suits me fine.
Which one is better? One sty for two swine,
Bad rat, bad cat...we're just the same sort.
We love filth, and so filth follows us.
We fly from honor, and honor abhors us
In this brothel where we are holding court.

Item: to Marion l'Idolle
And tall Jehanne of Britanny,
I give a license to teach school
Where students say what the course shall be.
This is the current theory,
Except in the prison at Mehun.
So take the school sign down, I say,
Since the trade has become so common.

Item: the next legacy
Is much deserved: Noel Jolis,
Two hundred strokes, no more than this,
With twigs cut from the willow tree
In my garden, this gift to be
At Henry's hands, Noel upended.
Chastisement is good charity,
Nobody should be offended.

Item: poor houses and the *Ostel*
Dieu...I'm not joking here:
Poor people have enough trouble.
Everyone sends them some leftover,
But the Mendicants lifted the cover
Of my goose, "just for a look,"
And all that's left is the rear
And the bones. The rest they took.

Item: my barber, Colin Galerne,
Near the herbalist, d'Angelot,
I leave a present from the Marne

Ung gros glasson (prins ou? en Marne),
Affin qu'a son ayse s'yverne.
De l'estomac le tiengne pres;
Se l'yver ainsi se gouverne,
Il aura chault l'esté d'après.

Item, riens aux Enfans Trouvez;
Mais les perdus faut que consolle.
Si doivent estre retrouvez,
Par droit, sur Marion l'Idolle.
Une leçon de mon escolle
Leur liray, qui ne dure guere.
Teste n'ayent dure ne folle;
Escoutent! car c'est la derniere.

Belle Leçon aux Enfants Perdus

"Beaulx enfans, vous perdez la plus
Belle rose de vo chappeau;
Mes clers pres prenans comme glus,
Se vous allez a Montpipeau
Ou a Rueil, gardez la peau:
Car, pour s'esbatre en ces deux lieux,
Cuidant que vaulsist le rappeau,
La perdit Colin de Cayeux.

"Ce n'est pas ung jeu de trois mailles,
Ou va corps, et peut estre l'ame.
Qui pert, riens n'y sont repentailles
Qu'on n'en meure a honte et diffame;
Et qui gaigne n'a pas a femme
Dido la royne de Cartage.
L'homme est donc bien fol et infame
Qui, pour si peu, couche tel gage.

For the winter, an ice floe,
To be kept close to his stomach, so
When summer comes around again
He'll be warm enough, and have no
Reason in the world to complain.

Item: for the Foundlings, nothing.
But the Lost Ones I must console.
They ought to be found again, and living,
By rights, with Marion l'Idolle.
I'll read them a lesson from my school.
I don't want them "hyperactive,"
Thick-headed, or playing the fool,
But listening. It's the last I'll give.

A Beautiful Lesson for Lost Children

"So you've a garland—good for you!
You could lose it all the same.
Clerks whose fingers stick like glue,
Now you'll want to try your game
At Montpipeau and Rueil. Don't blame
Me...that's a losing game you're in.
He thought he'd appeal and clear his name,
But Colin de Cayeux lost his skin.

It's not a children's game you're playing.
You risk the body, and maybe
The soul. The loser will be praying
For forgiveness, but die in infamy.
And the one who wins doesn't marry
The Queen of Carthage. He must be such
A hopeless case, or else he's crazy,
Who for so little risks so much.

"Qu'ung chascun encore m'escoute!
On dit, et il est vérité,
Que charreterie se boit toute,
Au feu l'yver, au bois l'esté:
S'argent avez, il n'est enté,
Mais le despendez tost et viste.
Qui en voyez vous herité?
Jamais mal acquest ne prouffite."

BALLADE
De Bonne Doctrine

"Car ou soies porteur de bulles,
Pipeur ou hasardeur de dez,
Tailleur de faulx coings et te brusles
Comme ceulx qui sont eschaudez,
Traistres parjurs, de foy vuidez;
Soies larron, ravis ou pilles:
Ou en va l'acquest, que cuidez?
Tout aux tavernes et aux filles.

"Ryme, raille, cymballe, luttes,
Comme fol, fainctif, eshontez;
Farce, brouille, joue des fleustes;
Fais, es villes et es citez,
Farces, jeux et moralitez;
Gaigne au berlanc, au glic, aux quilles:
Aussi bien va, or escoutez!
Tout aux tavernes et aux filles.

"De telz ordures te reculles,
Laboure, fauche champs et prez,
Sers et pense chevaux et mulles,
S'aucunement tu n'es lettrez;
Assez auras, se prens en grez.

Now, everyone, listen to me!
The money the wine-sellers get,
As the old saying goes, will be
Drunk up in the evening, every bit.
Money doesn't keep—you'll spend it
In no time. You'll not even see
The people it goes to. No profit
Comes of what is got dishonestly."

BALLADE
Of Good Doctrine

"Whether you're peddling a new bull,
Or you're a card sharp, or roll dice,
A counterfeiter, the kind they boil
In oil, a traitor who deals in lies,
A man with no faith, just a price,
Or one of the ordinary robbers,
Where's your money gone? Don't ask twice:
All to the taverns and the whores.

Rhyming, cymbals, flutes, and jokes
Used by shameless, lying clowns,
Sleight of hand, deception, hoax,
Playing in a village or a town
Farces, moralities, sword and crown...
Your gains with cards and dice, big scores,
Have disappeared, your wealth has flown,
All to the taverns and the whores.

If you think this a life for fools,
Labor in the field, plow and seed,
Service and groom horses and mules.
Though, as it happens, you can't read,
You earn enough for what you need.

Mais, se chanvre broyes ou tilles,
Ne tens ton labour qu'as ouvrez
Tout aux tavernes et aux filles?

"Chausses, pourpoins, esguilletez,
Robes, et toutes vos drappilles,
Ains que vous fassiez pis, portez
Tout aux tavernes et aux filles.

"A vous parle, compaings de galle:
Mal des ames et bien du corps,
Gardez vous tous de ce mau hasle
Qui noircist les gens quant sont mors;
Eschevez le, c'est ung mal mors;
Passez vous en mieulx que pourrez;
Et, pour Dieu, soiez tous recors
Qu'une fois viendra que mourrez."

Item, je donne aux Quinze Vings
(Qu'autant vauldroit nommer Trois Cens)
De Paris, non pas de Provins,
Car a eulx tenu je me sens;
Ilz auront, et je m'y consens,
Sans les estuys, mes grans lunettes,
Pour mettre a part, aux Innocens,
Les gens de bien des deshonnestes.

Icy n'y a ne ris ne jeu.
Que leur vault il avoir chevances,
N'en grans liz de parement jeu,
Engloutir vins en grosses pances,
Mener joye, festes et dances,
Et de ce prest estre a toute heure?
Toutes faillent telles plaisances,
Et la coulpe si en demeure.

But don't the wages of your labors—
Cleaning hemp, that's work indeed—
All go to the taverns and the whores?

Your fancy doublets and your hose,
Gowns once worn to loud applause,
Before they're nothing but old clothes,
Take them to the taverns and the whores."

I'm talking to you, my companions,
In body sound, in spirit sick:
Be careful to avoid the sun's
Burning that turns the body black.
It has an evil bite—stand back!
Try to live as well as you can,
And remember, for God's sake,
In time death comes to every man.

Item: I give the Fifteen Score
(You might as well say Three Hundred)
Of Paris, not Provins, to be sure,
For it's to Paris I'm connected,
The spectacles with which I read
And so judiciously reflected.
At the Innocents they'll know the dead
Who were good, from the...disaffected.

There's no matter here for laughing.
What did they gain by their riches,
Lying in beds of state and playing,
Gulping down wines, fattening paunches,
Running to festivals and dances,
Primed to be off at pleasure's call
To card games, intrigues, and romances?
All that remains is guilt, that's all.

Quant je considere ces testes
Entassees en ces charniers,
Tous furent maistres des requestes,
Au moins de la Chambre aux Deniers,
Ou tous furent portepanniers:
Autant puis l'ung que l'autre dire,
Car d'evesques ou lanterniers
Je n'y congnois rien a redire.

Et icelles qui s'enclinoient
Unes contre autres en leurs vies,
Desquelles les unes regnoient
Des autres craintes et servies,
La les voy toutes assouvies,
Ensemble en ung tas peslemesle:
Seigneuries leur sont ravies;
Clerc ne maistre ne s'y appelle.

Or sont ilz mors, Dieu ait leurs ames!
Quant est des corps, ilz sont pourris.
Aient esté seigneurs ou dames,
Souef et tendrement nourris
De cresme, fromentee ou riz,
Leurs os sont declinez en pouldre,
Auxquels ne chault d'esbatz ne ris.
Plaise au doulx Jhesus les absouldre!

Aux trespassez je fais ce laiz,
Et icelluy je communique
A regens, cours, sieges, palaiz,
Hayneurs d'avarice l'inique,
Lesquelz pour la chose publique
Se seichent les os et les corps:
De Dieu et de saint Dominique
Soient absols quant seront mors!

When I think of all the skulls
In charnel houses, piled in rows,
All of them were state officials...
Of the King's Household, I suppose.
Or carters and porters, who knows?
Which one of them was a bishop?
And which one could move a house
On his back with a strap? I give up.

And those heads once owned great lands,
And bowed and scraped to one another,
And gave other heads commands,
Who hastened to obey, in fear.
I see the heads now stacked up here
Pell-mell, estates torn from their hands.
From this decree there's no repair.
Who is the clerk now? Who commands?

God have their souls, now they are dead!
As for their bodies, they are rotting.
Though they were lords and ladies, fed
Richly on cream, rice, and milk pudding,
Their bones to dust are fast decaying,
Oblivious to sport and laughter.
May Jesus pardon them and bring
Them gently to His rest hereafter.

This legacy is for the dead,
For rulers, courts, and seats of justice.
I want the benefits extended
To those opposed to avarice;
Who, for the public good, the *res*,
Are wearing bone and body down.
God and Saint Dominic embrace
And pardon them when they pass on!

Item, riens a Jacquet Cardon,
Car je n'ay riens pour luy d'honneste,
Non pas que le gette habandon,
Sinon ceste bergeronnette;
S'elle eust le chant "Marionnette",
Fait pour Marion la Peautarde,
Ou d' "Ouvrez vostre huys, Guillemette",
Elle allast bien a la moustarde:

CHANSON

Au retour de dure prison,
Ou j'ai laissié presque la vie,
Se Fortune a sur moy envie,
Jugiez s'elle fait mesprison!
Il me semble que, par raison,
Elle deust bien estre assouvie
Au retour.

Se si plaine est de desraison
Que vueille que du tout devie,
Plaise a Dieu que l'ame ravie
En soit lassus en sa maison,
Au retour!

Item, donne a maistre Lomer,
Comme extraict que je suis de fee,
Qu'il soit bien amé (mais d'amer
Fille en chief ou femme coeffee,
Ja n'en ayt la teste eschauffee)
Et qu'il ne luy couste une noix
Faire ung soir cent fois la faffee,
En despit d'Ogier le Danois.

Item, donne aux amans enfermes,
Sans le laiz maistre Alain Chartier,
A leurs chevez, de pleurs et lermes

Item: to Jacquet Cardon, nothing.
Not that I'm likely to forget,
But I have nothing worth the giving.
Perhaps if this little song were set
To the tune of "Marionnette,"
Made for Marion la Peautarde,
Or "Open your door, Guillemette,"
It would serve to fetch the mustard.

SONG

On my return from prison
Where I very nearly died,
If Fortune would break my pride,
May she not be mistaken?
It seems to me that, in reason,
Fortune should be satisfied,
On my return.

If she be so far from reason
That she will not be denied,
Please God, let my soul be taken
To His house, and there abide,
On my return!

Item: to Master Lomer, that
He shall be loved, but should beware
Of those women who wear a hat
And those who go with the head bare...
Apart from that, not have a care,
And screw a hundred times a night,
More than the Tireless Dane, Ogier,
And pay nothing, not a mite.

For all pining lovers I want,
Beside Alain Chartier's legacy,
At their bedside a holy font

Trestout fin plain ung benoistier,
Et ung petit brain d'esglantier,
Qui soit tout vert, pour guipillon,
Pourveu qu'ilz diront ung psaultier
Pour l'ame du povre Villon.

Item, a maistre Jacques James,
Qui se tue d'amasser biens,
Donne fiancer tant de femmes
Qu'il vouldra; mais d'espouser, riens.
Pour qui amasse il? Pour les siens?
Il ne plaint fors que ses morceaulx:
Ce qui fut aux truyes, je tiens
Qu'il doit de droit estre aux pourceaulx.

Item, sera le Seneschal,
Qui une fois paya mes debtes,
En recompence, mareschal
Pour ferrer oes et canettes.
Je luy envoie ces sornettes
Pour soy desennuyer; combien,
S'il veult, face en des alumettes:
De bien chanter s'ennuye on bien.

Item, au Chevalier du Guet
Je donne deux beaulx petiz pages,
Philebert et le gros Marquet,
Qui tres bien servy, comme sages,
La plus grant partie de leurs aages,
Ont le prevost des mareschaulx.
Helas! s'ilz sont cassez de gages,
Aller les fauldra tous deschaulx.

Item, a Chappelain je laisse
Ma chappelle a simple tonsure,
Chargiee d'une seiche messe
Ou il ne fault pas grant lecture.
Resigné luy eusse ma cure,

Full of tears, and a sprig of rosemary
To sprinkle with, and let it be
Green. When I am dead and gone
They'll say a psalm in memory
Of the soul of poor François Villon.

Item: Master Jacques James, who
Is killing himself to pile wealth on:
He shall be affianced to
Many women, but marry none.
To whom will it go? A relation?
All he seems to care about is food,
Having enough. It's an obsession.
I've seen him eat. Scraps and bits. Pig food.

Item: because the Seneschal
Once paid for my extravagances,
I want him to be made a marshal
In charge of shoeing ducks and geese.
I'm sending him these pleasantries
To break the boredom. If he prefers,
Rolling them may make good matches.
Even good singing finally bores.

To the Chevalier du Guet
I leave two pretty little pages,
Philebert and Fat Marquet,
Who have served well as sages
The greater part of their ages,
Working for the Marshals' Provost.
Alas! They would have no wages,
And no shoes, if the job were lost.

Item: to Chappelain I pass
My chapel where just a tonsure
Is required, and a dry mass
With, perhaps, a brief lecture.
I'd also let him have my cure,

Mais point ne veult de charge d'ames;
De confesser, ce dit, n'a cure,
Sinon chamberieres et dames.

Pour ce que scet bien mon entente
Jehan de Calais, honnorable homme,
Qui ne me vit des ans a trente
Et ne scet comment je me nomme,
De tout ce testament, en somme,
S'aucun y a difficulté,
Oster jusqu'au rez d'une pomme
Je luy en donne faculté.

De le gloser et commenter,
De le diffinir et descripre,
Diminuer ou augmenter,
De le canceller et prescripre
De sa main et ne sceut escripre,
Interpreter et donner sens,
A son plaisir, meilleur ou pire:
A tout cecy je m'y consens.

Et s'aucun, dont n'ay congnoissance,
Estoit allé de mort a vie,
Je vueil et luy donne puissance,
Affin que l'ordre soit suyvie,
Pour estre mieulx parassouvie,
Que ceste aumosne ailleurs transporte,
Sans se l'appliquer par envie;
A son ame je m'en rapporte.

Item, j'ordonne a Sainte Avoye,
Et non ailleurs, ma sepulture;
Et, affin que chascun me voie,
Non pas en char, mais en painture,
Que l'on tire mon estature
D'ancre, s'il ne coustoit trop chier.

But he wouldn't want the care of souls,
Or confessions, unless they were
Those of chambermaids and girls.

Jehan de Calais knows my intent.
He's honorable, and has not seen me
In thirty years. If this *Testament*
Runs into any difficulty,
I give him full authority
To peel it down right to the core
Of what I surely must have meant.
That is what scholarship is for:

To misread, deconstruct, invent,
To prove the author asinine;
Dwell on a phrase you can augment
And ignore the opposite line,
Until your theory fits fine,
Interpreting and making sense
At your pleasure, excluding mine.
He has my entire confidence!

And if someone has crossed over
From death to life, and I not know,
I will and give that one power
To make others like him follow
The plan. I want my alms to go
To many, not some profiteer.
Let him see this done, that so
His conscience may be free and clear.

Item: I want my grave to be
At Sainte Avoye, not elsewhere,
So that everyone may see me,
Not in the flesh, as it were,
But in ink, a full-length picture,
If not too costly. Nothing more.

De tombel? riens: je n'en ay cure,
Car il greveroit le planchier.

Item, vueil qu'autour de ma fosse
Ce qui s'ensuit, sans autre histoire,
Soit escript en lettre assez grosse,
Et qui n'auroit point d'escriptoire,
De charbon ou de pierre noire,
Sans en riens entamer le plastre;
Au moins sera de moi memoire,
Telle qu'elle est d'ung bon follastre:

ÉPITAPHE

CY GIST ET DORT EN CE SOLLIER,
QU'AMOURS OCCIST DE SON RAILLON,
UNG POVRE PETIT ESCOLLIER,
QUI FUT NOMME FRANÇOYS VILLON.
ONCQUES DE TERRE N'EUT SILLON.
IL DONNA TOUT, CHASCUN LE SCET:
TABLES, TRESTEAULX, PAIN, CORBEILLON.
GALLANS, DICTES EN CE VERSET:

VERSET OU RONDEAU

REPOS ETERNEL DONNE A CIL,
SIRE, ET CLARTE PERPETUELLE,
QUI VAILLANT PLAT NI ESCUELLE
N'EUT ONCQUES, N'UNG BRAIN DE PERCIL.
IL FUT REZ, CHIEF, BARBE ET SOURCIL,
COMME UNG NAVET QU'ON RET OU PELLE.
REPOS ETERNEL DONNE A CIL

RIGUEUR LE TRANSMIT EN EXIL
ET LUY FRAPPA AU CUL LA PELLE,
NON OBSTANT QU'IL DIT: "J'EN APPELLE!"
QUI N'EST PAS TERME TROP SUBTIL.
REPOS ETERNEL DONNE A CIL.

A tomb? No, I don't think I care
For one. It might go through the floor.

Item: around the grave I want
This to be written, nothing grand,
But big enough letters. If tools can't
Be borrowed, let it be by hand,
In carbon or black stone, and
Careful not to bring the plaster down.
At least the memory will stand,
Such as it is, of a good clown:

EPITAPH

THIS HIGH VAULTED ROOM LOOKS DOWN
ON ONE WHOM LOVE KILLED WITH AN ARROW,
A POOR SCHOLAR, FRANÇOIS VILLON,
WHO NEVER HAD A FIELD OR FURROW,
BUT GAVE ALL, AS HIS FRIENDS WELL KNOW,
TABLE, BED, BREAKFAST, WILLINGLY.
SAY THIS VERSE FOR HIM BEFORE YOU GO,
FOR AS HE IS SO WILL YOU BE.

VERSE OR RONDEAU

GRANT HIM, LORD, YOUR PEACE ETERNAL,
AND YOUR LIGHT PERPETUALLY,
WHO HAD NO PLATE OR BOWL THAT HE
COULD CALL HIS OWN. HIS HEAD WAS ALL
SHAVED LIKE A TURNIP OR A BALL.
FOR WHAT REASON? DON'T ASK ME.
GRANT HIM, LORD, YOUR PEACE ETERNAL.

IN PRISON HE WAS CHAINED TO THE WALL
AND HIT IN THE ASS REPEATEDLY.
HE YELLED "I APPEAL!" WHICH COULD NOT BE
CLEARER, BUT HAD NO EFFECT AT ALL.
GRANT HIM, LORD, YOUR PEACE ETERNAL.

Item, je vueil qu'on sonne a bransle
Le gros beffroy, qui est de voirre;
Combien qu'il n'est cuer qui ne tremble,
Quant de sonner est a son erre.
Sauvé a mainte bonne terre,
Le temps passé, chascun le scet:
Fussent gens d'armes ou tonnerre,
Au son de luy, tout mal cessoit.

Les sonneurs auront quatre miches
Et, se c'est peu, demy douzaine;
Autant n'en donnent les plus riches,
Mais ilz seront de saint Estienne.
Vollant est homme de grant paine:
L'ung en sera; quant g'y regarde,
Il en vivra une sepmaine.
Et l'autre? Au fort, Jehan de la Garde.

Pour tout ce fournir et parfaire,
J'ordonne mes executeurs,
Auxquels fait bon avoir affaire
Et contentent biens leurs debteurs.
Ilz ne sont pas moult grans vanteurs
Et ont bien de quoy, Dieu mercis!
De ce fait seront directeurs.
Escry: je t'en nommerai six.

C'est maistre Martin Bellefaye,
Lieutenant du cas criminel.
Qui sera l'autre? G'y pensoye:
Ce sera sire Colombel;
S'il luy plaist et il luy est bel,
Il entreprendra ceste charge.
Et l'autre? Michiel Jouvenel.
Ces trois seulz, et pour tout, j'en charge.

Item: I would have it sounded,
The great bell in crystal cast,
Though there's no heart not filled with dread
When it rings. Its domain is vast.
Many good acres in ages past,
As everyone knows, it defended
From armed men or the tempest's blast.
At the sound all evil ended.

Four loaves should pay the ringers well.
If that's too few, then half a dozen.
The rich won't want to meet the bill,
But they'll do it for Saint Stephen.
Vollant is one of the working men:
He'll pitch in. Now that I consider,
He will live on that for seven
Days. Jehan de la Garde's another.

To plan and implement all this
I appoint my executors
Who are good men of business
And satisfy all their debtors—
They are not empty promisers,
And have money of their own,
Thank God!—to be the directors.
There are six. Write their names down.

First, Master Martin Bellefay,
Lieutenant of the Criminal Court
Who knows the ropes, in a way.
Who'll be after him? I thought
Master Colombel. He's a sport,
Game for anything he thinks will be
Pleasant and easy—he's that sort.
And Michiel Jouvenel. These three.

Mais, ou cas qu'ilz s'en excusassent,
En redoubtant les premiers frais,
Ou totallement recusassent,
Ceulx qui s'enssuivent cy après
Institue, gens de bien tres:
Phelip Brunel, noble escuyer,
Et l'autre, son voisin d'emprès,
Si est maistre Jaques Raguier,

Et l'autre, maistre Jaques James,
Trois hommes de bien et d'onneur,
Desirans de sauver leurs ames
Et doubtans Dieu Nostre Seigneur.
Plus tost y mettroient du leur
Que ceste ordonnance ne baillent;
Point n'auront de contrerolleur,
Mais a leur bon plaisir en taillent.

Des testamens qu'on dit le Maistre
De mon fait n'aura *quid* ne *quod;*
Mais ce sera ung jeune prestre,
Qui est nommé Thomas Tricot.
Voulentiers beusse a son escot,
Et qu'il me coustast ma cornete!
S'il sceust jouer a ung tripot,
Il eust de moy *le Trou Perrete.*

Quant au regart du luminaire,
Guillaume du Ru j'y commetz.
Pour porter les coings du suaire,
Aux executeurs le remetz.
Trop plus mal me font qu'oncques mais
Barbe, cheveulx, penil, sourcis.
Mal me presse, temps desormais
Que crie a toutes gens mercis.

In case they beg to be excused,
Fearing the initial expense,
Or absolutely have refused,
I empower, hereby and hence,
Three fine men of my acquaintance:
Philippe Brunel, esquire,
And his neighbor across the fence,
Master Jacques Reguier,

And Jacques James. Each of the three
Is an honorable gentleman
And solid man of property,
Seeking his soul's salvation.
He'd rather sacrifice his own
Than fail to keep this ordinance.
He'll have no controller looking on
But do exactly as he wants.

The so-called Master Will, probate,
Will get neither *quid* nor *quod* of mine.
To handle this I designate
Thomas Tricot, a young divine.
I'd drink gladly if he would sign
Although it might cost me my hat.
If he knew how to play the baseline
I'd let him have the *Trou Perrete*.

The lanterns for my funeral
Guillaume du Ru will provide.
As for who will bear the pall,
The executors must decide.
More than ever I am being tried
By beard, hair, groin, and eyebrow,
A pain that I can scarcely bide.
I ask everyone to pardon me now.

BALLADE
De Mercy

A Chartreux et a Celestins,
A Mendians et a Devotes,
A musars et claquepatins,
A servans et filles mignotes
Portans surcotz et justes cotes,
A cuidereaux d'amours transsis
Chaussans sans meshaing fauves botes,
Je crie a toutes gens mercis.

A filletes monstrans tetins
Pour avoir plus largement d'ostes,
A ribleurs, mouveurs de hutins,
A bateleurs, traynans marmotes,
A folz, folles, a sotz et sotes,
Qui s'en vont siflant six a six,
A marmosetz et mariotes,
Je crie a toutes gens mercis.

Sinon aux traistres chiens mastins
Qui m'ont fait rongier dures crostes
Maschier mains soirs et mains matins,
Qu'ores je ne crains pas trois crotes.
Je feisse pour eulx petz et rotes;
Je ne puis, car je suis assis.
Au fort, pour eviter riotes,
Je crie a toutes gens mercis.

Qu'on leur froisse les quinze costes
De gros mailletz, fors et massis,
De plombes et telz pelotes.
Je crie a toutes gens mercis.

BALLADE
For Pardon

Carthusians, Celestines,
Mendicants, layabouts,
Filles Dieu, fashion queens,
House servants, prostitutes,
Surcoats, form-fitting suits,
The mad with love putting on,
Without complaining, fawn boots,
I ask everyone for pardon.

Whores who show you their tits
When shades of eve begin to fall,
The thief who solitary sits,
Men who start a barroom brawl,
Showmen with a monkey, and all
Farceurs and clowns, half a dozen
In a group who shout and whistle,
I ask everyone for pardon.

Except for dogs who like to bite,
Who made me gnaw crusts, dry bits,
Every day, morning and night,
For whom now I don't give three shits.
I'd fart for them and belch, but it's
Impossible, I'm sitting down.
However, to call it quits,
I ask everyone for pardon.

Smash their fifteen ribs with swings
Of heavy mallets, massive and strong,
Lead balls, and other such playthings.
I ask everyone for pardon.

AUTRE BALLADE

Icy se clost le testament
Et finist du povre Villon,
Venez a son enterrement,
Quant vous orrez le carrillon,
Vestus rouge com vermillon,
Car en amours mourut martir;
Ce jura il sur couillon,
Quant de ce monde voult partir.

Et je croy bien que pas n'en ment;
Car chassié fut comme ung souillon
De ses amours hayneusement,
Tant que, d'icy a Roussillon,
Brosse n'y a ne brossilon
Qui n'eust, ce dit il sans mentir,
Ung lambeau de son cotillon,
Quant de ce monde voult partir.

Il est ainsi et tellement,
Quant mourut n'avoit qu'ung haillon;
Qui plus, en mourant, mallement
L'espoignoit d'Amours l'esguillon;
Plus agu que le ranguillon
D'ung baudrier luy faisoit sentir
C'est de quoy nous esmerveillon,
Quant de ce monde voult partir.

Prince, gent comme esmerillon,
Sachiez qu'il fist au departir:
Ung traict but de vin morillon,
Quant de ce monde voult partir.

ANOTHER BALLADE

The Testament comes to an end...
With it, the life of poor Villon.
In case you're planning to attend
His funeral, there's the carillon.
He's robed in red, vermilion,
A martyr to love, as he swore
On one testicle when he passed on
To a better life than he had before.

And I believe he did not lie.
He was driven from love's mansion
By hate. I say this truthfully,
From here as far as Roussillon
There wasn't a bush that didn't have on
A bit of rag stained with his gore.
His friends all hope that now he's gone
To a better life than he had before.

This is why, at the end of his life,
He owned just one piece of clothing,
And that's not all. Love with his knife
Gave him a stab as he lay dying.
This pain, he said, was more trying
Than a belt buckle. A metaphor?
We found his sayings mystifying
On leaving the life he had before.

Prince, as gentle as a falcon,
You ought to know one thing more:
He put a pichet of red wine down,
Then left the life that he had before.

Notes

THE LEGACY

Page 2. Villon says *"de sens rassis"* (of sound mind). I have translated this as "no bites or kicks" in order to rhyme with "fifty-six" in the opening line. "No bites or kicks" is in the same horsy idiom as Villon's *"Le frain aux dens"* (bit in my teeth).

3. *Vegetius*: Flavius Vegetius Renatus, fourth-century Roman author of a work on the art of war, *De re militari,* that was much admired.

When Christmas came: Villon says that he finished writing *The Legacy* at Christmas. It is the dead of winter—his ink has frozen and his candle gone out. The records show that at Christmas Villon met Guy Tabarie, a clerk, and they proceeded to the *Mule* where they had supper with Nicolas, a monk from Picardy, Colin de Cayeux, the son of a locksmith, and Petit Jehan, a "picklock." They were planning a burglary, with Villon as director of the operation.

There was a coffer at the College of Navarre where the community kept their funds. The five first entered the house of a M. Saint-Simon by going over a low wall. There they left their cloaks with Tabarie to guard, and proceeded to the College. They climbed over a high wall. This would have been at close to ten o'clock. In the account Tabarie gave months later when he was questioned, the others returned at midnight with a little canvas bag containing gold *écus* they had stolen. They threatened to kill him if he told what he'd seen, and gave him ten *écus* for guarding their clothes, and split the money among them, more than a hundred *écus* each.

On March 9-10, 1457 an enquiry into the robbery was set on foot. It was a serious enquiry, with many important people taking part. They examined the locks and said that the thieves could not have been very professional. The theft must have taken place two or three months ago. But the thieves were still on the run and, Champion says, who knows if it would ever have been discovered if Guy Tabarie had not talked, volubly, to a man he met?[5]

On the night before Christmas Villon was climbing over walls

---

5. Pierre Champion, *François Villon: Sa Vie et Son Temps. II.* (Paris: Librairie Honoré Champion, 1967), 40-44.

and helping Nicolas, Colin de Cayeux, and Petit Jehan pick locks, or perhaps he was giving directions. In *Le Lais* he shows himself during these hours sitting in his room, writing *Le Lais*. Could it be that he wrote these stanzas after the robbery at the College in order to provide himself with an alibi?

I saw her standing in plain sight: Jean Favier thinks that this refers to Katherine de Vausselles, the woman Villon names in *The Testament*. She was Villon's "great love ... and never responded with anything but sarcasms, snubs, even blows."[6]

On the other hand, David Mus says that the opening of *Le Lais* is fiction. The woman the poet says he saw "standing in plain sight" is fictional, "especially after Villon has taken pains to draw us so far from reality, and by his disjointed (*saccadés*) changes of style, to place us on a plane of complete artificiality." In these opening stanzas Villon is parodying the rhetoric of courtly love, from which he has to escape in order to write poetry in his own, original style."[7]

The style at the beginning of *Le Lais* is certainly a parody of the rhetoric of courtly love, but this does not preclude its drawing on real events. Villon has taken part in the robbery of the College of Navarre. He has come under suspicion and may find himself in the Châtelet, being "questioned," that is, tortured to obtain a confession. The outcome is unpredictible. He plans to leave Paris in a hurry for some place where the law will not find him.

He cannot write about the real reason he is leaving. So he turns fact into fiction. For a dungeon at the Châtelet he substitutes "the darkest dungeon, love"—a woman he loved has betrayed him and he has to end the unhappy affair. This is the reason he is leaving Paris. He is using the clichés of the literature of courtly love, but there is an urgency in the writing, a fear, that strikes me as real. A lover being treated cruelly by his mistress was common in this literature, and the high-flown style is a parody, but his having to escape sounds true. *Le Lais* begins with a parody, but it is parody with a ring of truth.

Like horses with white feet: Horses with white feet could pass tolls

---

6. Jean Favier, *François Villon* (Paris: Librairie Arthème Fayard, 1982), 471-472.
7. David Mus, *La Poétique de François Villon* (Paris: Librairie Armand Colin, 1967; Editions Champ Villon, 1992), 107.

without paying, and so were said to promise more than they performed. King Louis XI said to the Duke of Alençon, "Godfather, godfather, do not fail me in my need; do not behave like the horse with white feet."[8]

planting: copulating: The narrator then says that he will "strike upon another die" (*frapper un ung autre coing*). I have not included this phrase, for it repeats what he has just said and takes up needed space.

5. *my very life's in danger:* He is not exaggerating. His life would be in danger if it were proved that he took part in the robbery of the College of Navarre. Criminals who were deemed "incorrigible" were hanged, and Villon had killed a man and been banished from Paris. When, some years later, he was condemned to be hanged—he appealed, and the sentence was changed to banishment—he was innocent of any wrongdoing. He had only been present at a brawl in the street. As he says in *Le Testament,* there were those who, if they could, would not allow him to live.

I'm going to Angers: Villon had an uncle in Angers, an old monk who was said to be rich. He may have intended to rob him, acting as a spy for the Coquillards. Guy Tabarie was questioned at the Châtelet about the robbery of the College of Navarre. He stated, in his deposition of July 22, 1458, that he told Pierre Marchant in April 1457 that Villon was going to Angers to rob his uncle.

The Coquillards were a loose organisation of thieves, counterfeiters, crooks and cheats of all kinds who operated throughout France. Was Villon one of these professional criminals? Champion says that it is hard to argue that he wasn't. *(II,* 70-71) Villon had close friends who associated with the Coquillards, notably Regnier de Montigny and Colin de Cayeux, and he wrote some poems using their thieves' argot. (On the other hand, it has been suggested that he picked up the argot at one remove, from Colin de Cayeux.) The extent of Villon's involvement with the Coquillards remains problematic.

no herring swimming in the sea: There has been some controversy

---

8. Maurice Allem, *François Villon, Oeuvres Complètes* (Grenoble, Paris: B. Arthaud, 1947), 157.

over this herring. One may take the word "*Dont*" to refer to the narrator, whose "*umeur*" (state of mind) has changed for the worse—he has been hung out by his mistress to dry like a herring at Boulogne. Or "*Dont*" may refer to the lover who has supplanted him in her favor. This man is well fed and therefore as amorous as a herring. There is another possible reading, from a different text, which Sargent-Baur translates:

> Another man is in the scene
> Whose money makes a louder clink,
> Younger than I, more cheerful too.[9]

7. *Guillaume Villon*: His adoptive father. The narrator is going to leave his reputation, and his tents and pavilion, to this respected man, a chaplain and professor of canon law who lives in the cloister of Saint Benoît. The reader is surely aware that nothing the narrator says is to be taken at face value. By this time his reputation is anything but good—he killed Philippe Sermoise in a street fight. He doesn't have tents and a pavilion, nor any of the other articles of value he is bequeathing: diamond, coat of mail, and so on. With few exceptions, his bequests hold the recipients up to ridicule.

Guillaume de Villon, whom the poet calls his "more than father," ought to be one of the exceptions. But is he? Champion relates the story of a child who had the habit of stealing—his father only laughed at it. The child continued to steal until the man was caught and condemned to death. When he was led to the gibbet he asked the favor of being allowed to kiss his father. He bit off his nose. (*I*, 33)

10. *Ythier Marchant*: A boyhood friend of Villon who came of a rich family. He was involved in Burgundian politics—King Louis XI said he was the man he most hated. The King bought his loyalty, but Marchant took part in a plot to poison the King, and died in prison in 1474. "*Branc*" means short sword, but it also suggests "*bran*," excrement. There is another possible meaning: the word

---

9. Barbara N. Sargent-Baur, *François Villon, Complete Poems, Edited with English Translations and Commentary* (Toronto: University of Toronto Press, 1994), 23.

"*branc*" in the jargon of Paris meant an erect penis. Favier says that the woman who was Villon's "great love," Katherine de Vausselles, became Marchant's mistress (471-477). Leaving him a "branc" would be an insult to them both.

Jehan le Cornu: He too came of a rich family, financiers. He worked in the equivalent of the Treasury, then as criminal clerk at the Châtelet. He died of the plague in 1476.

Saint Amant: Pierre de Saint-Amant held an important position as Clerk of the Treasury. Such men rode horses, so the poet wills him a horse and mule, from tavern signs. The horse stands still because Saint Amant is impotent. "*She-Mule*" would imply a sterile woman, and from what Villon says in *The Testament* this would be Saint Amant's wife, whom he dislikes. There must be a reason for the "*Zebra*" pulling backward that we do not know.

Blarru: Jean de Blarru was a goldsmith with a shop on the Pont-au-Change. A surprising amount of information about the Paris of Villon's day, and the men and women he knew, has been unearthed by scholars. (We know comparatively little about the life of Chaucer who died in 1400, or Shakespeare, d. 1616.) There has also been a considerable amount of speculation by those who have written about Villon. It is said that Blarru may have been engaged in a lawsuit over a diamond.

Omnis utriusque sexus: In 1215 the church decreed that all Christians must confess at least once a year. In 1409 the Mendicants (wandering friars) received the right from Pope Nicholas V to hear confessions. This was opposed by the regular clergy, but in 1449 the right of the Mendicants was reaffirmed by a bull. Villon is opposed to Mendicant orders such as the Carmelites—he attacks them repeatedly for being greedy, lecherous, and scheming. Here he is leaving the clergy the old 1215 decree that gave them the sole right to hear confessions.

9. Robert Valée: (Or Vallée) He may have been at the University with Villon. Like le Cornu, Valée came of a family of financiers, and he was hardly the poor clerk Villon says he is—he was a prosecutor in Parliament. The offer to buy him a stall is just an insult. "*Trumillières*" were greaves, leg armor, here referring to a tavern sign. The name Jehanneton de Millieres appears in a register of Parliament.

Decent, hard working, country bred: Villon says only that Valée came of a "good background" (*de lieu honneste*). I am very unwilling to add to or excise words an author has written, but in translating verse it is essential to imitate the form—in these poems a stanza rhyming ababbcbc. I have inserted this line in order to rhyme. I think Villon might have found the line acceptable, for it elaborates on "*de lieu honneste*" as he might have done, giving Valée a humble background that would show up the pretensions of his family. They were not "country bred"—they were city people, wealthy financiers.

Art of Memory: A book on self-improvement. They had them in those days too.

by Easter: The year ran from Easter Sunday to Holy Saturday.

Jacques Cardon: A dealer in cloth and clothing who wouldn't have needed the gloves and cape Villon is leaving him. And there is no such thing as an acorn from a willow tree. As acorns were fed to pigs, perhaps this suggests that Cardon ate like a pig.

11. *Regnier de Montigny* came of a "noble family" that had become impoverished. Montigny and Villon were clerks, that is, clerics—they were being educated for positions in the church. They were companions in youthful escapades, then each of them took up with bad company. At the end of 1455 Montigny was reported to be a card sharp and one of the Coquillards, involved in their underworld of crooks and thieves. He was committed three times to the Châtelet and released to the Bishop of Paris, without mending his ways.

Clerks could appeal to the ecclesiastical authorities—to discipline clerks was one of their privileges. Those sentenced in a civil court could appeal to their bishop, be remanded, and win a lighter sentence. The privilege was frequently abused: robbers and counterfeiters escaped hanging. As a result, the local authority might ignore an appeal.

Montigny was committed to prison at Tours, Rouen, and Bordeaux. Then he stole a chalice from the Church of Saint Jean en Grève—an act of sacrilege. This time he was not remanded to the Bishop of Paris. He was condemned by the lay tribunal to be "hanged and strangled." All the efforts of his family, even a letter of remission from the King, failed to move the city council. Regnier de Montigny was hanged in Paris in 1457, less than a year after Villon wrote these lines. (Villon had another friend who would be hanged,

Colin de Cayeux. Villon took part with Cayeux in the robbery of the College of Navarre.)

Jehan Raguier: A sergeant of the Twelve, the guard of the Provost of Paris.

Seigneur de Grigny: Philippe Brunel, a petty nobleman who claimed the lordship of Grigny. He was quarrelsome and generally detested. Villon bequeaths him Nijon and Vicestre (Bicêtre), "two ruinous castles to oversee." (Sargent-Baur 137)

devil's whelp, Mouton: We don't know who Mouton was. Villon calls him a *"chanjon,"* a changeling, the child of a demon that has been substituted for a human child.

Jacques Raguier: Perhaps the son of Charles VII's cook. The Abruvouër Popin, on the right bank of the Seine, was a watering place for horses; the *Pomme de Pin*, a tavern on the Ile de la Cité. "To plant" could mean to joke, but here, as on page 3, means to copulate. I have added "dace" to the menu in order to rhyme.

Jehan Mautaint, Pierre Basanier, et al: Mautaint was the Examiner at the Châtelet; shortly after this was written he would investigate the robbery of the College of Navarre. Basanier was a notary at the Châtelet and would be promoted to criminal clerk. The "seigneur" who put down disturbances so firmly was the Provost, Robert d'Estouteville, head of the Paris police. He protected Villon when he might have been arrested, and Villon will include in *The Testament* a ballade for d'Estouteville. He seems to have been sincerely grateful: the ballade oozes flattery at every pore.

Fournier: Pierre Fournier was not Villon's personal lawyer, as Villon says he is. Fournier "represented the community of Saint Benoît at the Châtelet."[10]

13. *Jehan Trouvé*: A butcher's assistant who had run-ins with the law.

The Sheep, The Crowned Ox, The Cow, The Helmet, The Lantern in rue Pierre au Let, and *Three Lilies* were tavern signs.

The Captain of the Watch: Jean de Harlay was Captain of the Watch.

---

10. Anthony Bonner, *The Complete Works of François Villon, Translated, with a Biography and Notes* (New York: Bantam Books, 1960), 188.

For this post you had to be a knight, the symbol of which was a helmet. Someone was disputing Harlay's claim to the post, so Villon bequeaths him a helmet.

I'll take Three Lilies: The word "*lis*" could mean "beds" as well as lilies. There weren't any beds in the dungeons at the Châtelet, the prison to which Villon says he may be sent.

Perrenet Marchant: Pierre Marchant was the constable at the Châtelet. Straw was used there for mattresses. The word "*merchant*" could also mean pimp, so he could use the bales of straw for that too.

Loup, Cholet: Jean le Loup and Casin Cholet were river policemen on the Seine. It seems they were also thieves with whom Villon went duck-hunting. Loup and Cholet stole firewood and coal unloaded off the boats. The long cloaks would serve for concealment, but the boots with no uppers wouldn't keep their feet dry.

15. *the little ones*: These were Colin Laurens, Girart Gossouyn, and Jehan Marceau, three rich old usurers who were generally detested. Marceau was an enemy of d'Estouteville, Villon's protector.

four blancs: Coins of little value.

The children will have hearty meals: It was worms that would have had the meals. The three "little ones" would have been buried long ago.

Guillaume Cotin, Thibault de Victry: Two old canons of Notre Dame. They were rich and had held important posts in the government. "Villon's church of Saint Benoît had been involved in an ecclesiastical quarrel with the chapter of Notre Dame, which was one more reason for Villon's detesting these old codgers." (Bonner 189)

Guillot Gueuldry: A house in rue Saint Jacques called "la maison Guillot Gueutry" had been rented to Laurent Gueuldry, "a butcher who owed stall rent to Saint Benoît and land rent to Notre Dame (and never paid either rent)." (Sargent-Baur 223) This legacy, like others, is worthless.

17. *The cross that's painted in the sign*: The commentators haven't been able to explain this stanza. The cross in rue Saint Anthoine could mark a bishop's residence, or indicate that the house has a billiard table or croquet mallets; a pot of water from the Seine would be indescribably filthy; pigeons in jail would be prisoners, and perhaps a mirror would be needed so they could shave. The goodwill of

the jailer's wife? What is to be inferred from this is anybody's guess.

the Mendicant: There were four orders of Mendicant friars: Dominicans (also called Jacobins), Francisans, Carmelites, and Augustinians. For Villon's opinion of the Mendicants, see the note on *Omnis utriusque sexus,* page 7.

The Filles Dieu, and the Beguine: The Filles Dieu were an order of nuns who cared for the sick; the Beguine, nuns whose vows were not perpetual. Bonner calls them "lay nuns."

To preach on signs: Fifteen signs would signal the approach of the Last Judgment. The friars often preached on this topic.

19. *Jehan, grocer*: Jehan de la Garde, not a modern-day grocer but a dealer in spices. Condiments were ground in a pestle, so Villon leaves him a mortar of gold as his sign—the grocer was wealthy—and for a pestle leaves him one of the votive crutches left by pilgrims to Saint Maur, who helped people with gout.

Burn, Saint Anthony: Erysipelas, an epidemic disease, was called Saint Anthony's Fire. We don't know the nature of the "misery" Villon says this man caused him.

Merebeuf, Nicolas de Louviers, the Prince, Gouvieux: Pierre Merebeuf was a draper in the rue des Lombards, Nicolas de Louviers a city magistrate and tax collector. The Prince is the Prince of Fools who rode in a procession and threw cardboard coins to the crowd, in the manner of the King who, on his state appearances, threw real coins. The village of Gouvieux was situated to the north of Paris, near Chantilly.

Pierre de Rousseville: A concierge who may have had some connection with the Châtelet.

The Sorbonne bell: Villon lived only a few hundred feet from the cloister of Saint Benoît where Guillaume de Villon lived, and where *The Legacy* was probably written. (Champion I, 141-143)

The promise that the angel made: The angelus, a devotion of the Western church that, at noon and in the evening, commemorates the incarnation.

21. *the estimative/ Provides prospective*: Villon is holding scholastic terms up to ridicule, the way Molière pokes fun at the jargon of the medical profession. But Mus speaks of the "perfect psychological realism" of this last scene in *Le Lais.* He says, "We are not at all sure that this passage is as comic as has been supposed.... In parodying

the rhetoric of love Villon showed this to be practically useless; by his use of scholastic jargon he shows us the kind of poetry that he proposes to substitute for it." (Mus 119)

THE TESTAMENT

In the summer of 1461 Villon was in prison at Mehun-sur-Loire, for a crime the nature of which we do not know, but it must have been serious, for he was imprisoned in a dungeon, with his legs shackled, living on bread and water. He was fortunate, however: on October 2 the newly crowned king, Louis XI, on his way from Paris to his residences in the Val de Loire passed through Mehun and liberated the prisoners. Villon would express his gratitude to the king in a hymn dedicated to Princess Marie. He was free but broken in health. After leaving Mehun he came to Moulins, "a good town that had the gift of hope." Moulins was the seat of the Duke of Bourbon whose emblem was "Hope."

> In my misfortunes, penniless,
> God who spoke so cheeringly
> To two on the way to Emmaus
> Also showed me a fine city...

If he were hoping to be noticed and treated favorably by the Duke he was disappointed. The Duke remained unaware of his existence. This was just as well, considering Villon's prison record.

From Moulins Villon returned to Paris. This was dangerous—he was wanted for his part in the robbery of the College of Navarre. He wrote *The Testament* while in hiding, either in Paris or the suburbs. Then he went back to his room in the cloister of Saint Benoît. In early November he was in prison once again, at the Châtelet, for a crime that must not have been grave, for he was about to be set free when the attorney of the Faculty of Theology objected. He was held at the Châtelet for his complicity in the robbery of the College. He engaged to reimburse the College 120 gold *écus* in three years, and was released.

In November of 1462, Villon had supper with three friends and was returning with them to his room. They passed an open window at which an attorney and his scribes were working. One of Villon's companions spat in their ink. They didn't think it was funny—they ran out and a fight ensued. The attorney was stabbed—in the hand, not a serious wound. Villon had nothing to do with the wounding, it seems he kept his distance, but he was recognized and brought to trial. He was condemned to be hanged—an incredible miscarriage of justice! He appealed, and the death sentence was set aside, but he was banished from Paris for ten years. This is the last we see of François Villon. Nothing more is known of his life.

Page 23. *Bishop Thibault d'Aussigny*: Bishop of Orléans and lord of the Chastellany of Mehun-sur-Loire. He was also, as Villon says, "Bishop of the Streets"—in public processions he made the sign of the cross over the crowd. Thibault had Villon shackled and kept him on bread and water. Villon was a *clerc* (cleric) in a minor order, and subject to the discipline of the Bishop of Paris. This is why he says that Thibault isn't his bishop, implying that Thibault has exceeded his authority. Villon probably appealed his sentence at Mehun-sur-Loire. Such appeals, however, might be overruled or simply ignored: "He thought he'd appeal and clear his name,/ But Colin de Cayeux lost his skin." Who would want to intercede and possibly antagonize the "Bishop of the Streets" on behalf of a minor cleric who had committed a crime?

we should pray/ For those who hate us: Matthew 5:44. "Love your enemies, bless them that curse you, do good to them that hate you..." Also Luke 6:27-28. *The Holy Bible*, Authorized (King James) Version.

"I will repay": Romans 12:19. "Vengeance is mine; I will repay, saith the Lord."

25. *the late Cotart*: Jehan Cotart, a prosecutor for the diocese, died on January 9, 1461. All we know about him is what Villon tells us: Cotart was a heavy drinker—see the ballade on page 101.

a Picard's prayer: People in Picardy had been accused of heresy. Some made up prayers of their own, others rejected any kind of prayer as useless. In saying a Picard's prayer for Bishop Thibault, Villon may be saying nothing at all.

In the "Deus Laudem": In Villon's time psalms were identified by the opening words, not by number. The psalm Villon refers to is Psalm 108 in the Vulgate, Psalm 107 in the Protestant Bible. He refers us to the seventh verse. If we take "Deus laudem" as the first verse, then the seventh reads, "May his days be few; and his bishopric let another take." This applies exactly to Bishop Thibault d'Aussigny, that is, Villon's feelings about the Bishop.

There is another way to count the verses that gives us, instead, "When he is judged, may he go out condemned, and may his prayer be turned to sin." But a reader in the fifteenth century copied out, between the stanzas in a manuscript of Villon's poem, "May his days be few; and his bishopric let another take." This must be the verse Villon meant.

Louis, the good King: Louis XI passed through Mehun on October 2, 1461, and granted the prisoners their freedom.

Jacob's happiness: The patriarch Jacob had twelve sons. (Genesis 35:22)

Like Methusaleh: Methusaleh lived 969 years. (Genesis 5:27)

27. *Charlemagne*: King of the Franks (768-814 A.D.) and Western (Holy Roman) Emperor (800-814 A.D.)

Saint Martial: Villon wishes Louis to be "bons." When said of rulers or military men, "bon" meant brave. But Saint Martial wasn't martial except in name. I have made him "bon" in his religion. He was Bishop of Limoges in the third century.

the Dauphin: Villon says "feu Dauphin" (the late Dauphin). Louis had been the Dauphin and now was King of France.

Averroës: Ibn Rushd, a Spanish Arab physician and philosopher who wrote commentaries on Aristotle.

29. *In my misfortunes, penniless*: Villon says "cheminant sans croix ni pille," journeying without cross or obverse. That is, without heads or tails: without a coin.

on the way to Emmaus: After the Crucifixion two disciples on their way to Emmaus were joined by the risen Christ. (Luke 24:13-31)

That held a gift of hope for me: Villon is probably referring to Moulins, where he came after leaving Mehun-sur-Loire. Moulins was the capital of Burgundy and seat of the Duke whose motto was "Esperance" (Hope). But Villon was not brought to the Duke's attention, either for better or worse.

Not just sinning but keeping on: obduracy, persisting in sin, is a common theme in Christian theology.

The Romance of the Rose: An allegorical poem begun in the thirteenth century, c. 1237, by Guillaume de Lorris and continued in the fourteenth century by Jean de Meun. It was widely read. However, the passage Villon refers to, about forgiving youthful indiscretions, is not in this work but in Jean de Meun's *Testament*.

31. *the great Alexander's reign*: Alexander, King of Macedonia, 336-323 B.C. Villon attributes this story to Valerius Maximus, a first century Roman historian. He is probably confusing him with the fourth century Julius Valerius who wrote an *Epitome* of legends about Alexander.

Diomedes: The pirate has no "historicity"—he is probably a fictitious character.

35. *"Rejoice in youth"*: Ecclesiastes 11:9. "Rejoice, O young man, in thy youth..."

a dish that's very different: "put away evil from thy flesh: for childhood and youth are vanity." (Ecclesiastes 11:10)

The weaver has a straw: "My days are swifter than a weaver's shuttle, and are spent without hope." (Job 7:6) Villon has changed the image from cutting a thread to burning it with a straw. Sargent-Baur suggests that he may have remembered *succiditur* (is cut) as *succenditur* (is burnt)... "or he may have substituted an observed gesture for the biblical words." The lines about not fearing death are not in Job: they are Villon's.

37. *Of Celestines or of Chartreux*: Celestines were a religious order founded by Pope Celestine in the thirteenth century. They had a house in Paris. Chartreux (Carthusians) were Benedictines, organized in the eleventh century by Saint Bruno of Cologne. They lived outside Paris. Villon suggests that these members of "a holy band" are opportunists and hypocrites, "In high boots, prayer book in hand."

39. *And what I have written, let it stay*: He is not a judge, and hopes that the rich will be forgiven their transgressions, but he wants what he has written about them to be left just as it is. *Stet.*

Let's leave the church where it is placed: Let's leave preaching to the church.

Jacques Coeur: "without doubt the most spectacular businessman of the Middle Ages." (Bonner 193) From humble origins Coeur rose to being one of the wealthiest individuals France has ever seen. He held important government posts, was master of the mint under Charles VII, and lent his own money to the government during the Hundred Years' War. Many members of the court were heavily in debt to him. Accused of poisoning the king's mistress, Coeur escaped from France. He was on his way to fight the Turks when he died, "at Chios on the 25th of November, 1456, just one month before Villon wrote *The Legacy*."

41. *psalms of David*: "As for man, his days are as grass . . . the place thereof shall know it no more." (Psalm 103:15-16.)

preacher's: He probably has in mind itinerant preachers such as the Dominicans.

with-her collar-turned-up lady: Wearing upturned collars lined with fur was high fashion. Ordinances prohibited prostitutes from wearing them, to comply with church censures of vanity, but also so that ladies of fashion could be distinguished from prostitutes. Villon also mentions "*atours*," conical hats worn by noblewomen, and "*bourreletz*," headdresses lined with horsehair, with an attached hood—a bourgeois fashion. There wasn't room for this line in my translation.

Paris, or Helen's death: In the legends on which the Homeric poems are based, Paris, the son of Priam, King of Troy, carried off Helen, the wife of Menelaus, King of Sparta. This was the cause of the Trojan War.

43. *Flora*: In Plutarch and Juvenal, a Roman courtesan. Flora may have been a generic name.

Archipiada: Apparently Villon heard the name Alcibiades and assumed that, because Alcibiades was said to be a model of beauty, Alcibiades was a woman. He was an Athenian general and statesman of the fifth century B.C.

Thais: Either a Greek courtesan of the fourth century B.C., the mistress of Alexander the Great, or an Egyptian courtesan converted to Christianity by the monk Paphnutius. Perhaps the two are conflated. (Sargent-Baur 331)

Echo: A Nymph whose chattering prevented Hera from surprising her husband Zeus among the Nymphs. Hera punished Echo: she would be able to speak only when someone else spoke first.

Heloise . . . Pierre Abelard: Abelard, a philosopher and theologian, was entrusted by Fulbert, a canon at Notre Dame, with the education of Fulbert's niece Heloise. Abelard married her secretly. Fulbert had Abelard castrated. Abelard became a monk, and Heloise a nun.

Buridan: A fourteenth century professor at the University of Paris. It was said that the Queen of France and Navarre would invite students to her palace on the Seine, give them a fine dinner, sleep with them, and have them tossed in the river and drowned. Buridan got himself invited and stayed with her for three days. He had arranged for some students to be passing with a barge full of hay when the time came for him to be dropped in the river. They dropped a rock instead. The Queen was deceived and Buridan was saved.

The real Buridan was only five years old when Jeanne de Navarre was Queen. The account of their affair is a mythic representation of the cycle of the seasons. See Mus's exegesis of the ballade of "the snows of yesterday," paraphrased briefly in the Preface to this book. The famous ballade is not, as used to be thought, about beautiful women vanishing like snow. Snow was by no means beautiful in the Middle Ages—it came with winter, the season of cold and death. And the women named in the ballade were not all known for their beauty. What they represent is the regenerative principle in nature. Placing Buridan in the sack is symbolic of sexual intercourse.

Queen Blanche: Blanche of Castille, the mother of Louis IX. Sargent-Baur comments: "her musical talents are not attested."

Bertha Bigfoot, Beatrice, Alice: Bertha Bigfoot may be the wife of Pépin le Bref and mother of Charlemagne, or else she is the Bertha who was wife of King Robert and punished by God for an incestuous marriage. She gave birth to a son with the head and neck of a goose, and her right foot was changed into the foot of a goose. In folklore names and people get mixed up. Beatrice and Alice were generic names for women who had love affairs.

Arembourg: The wife of Foulques d'Anjou. She died in 1126.

Joan: Joan of Arc. Burned as a witch by the English in 1431.

45. *Calixtus*: Pope Calixtus III, d. 1458.

Alfonso: King Alfonso V of Aragon, d. 1458.

Duke of Bourbon: Charles I, d. 1456.

Arthur: Arthur III, Duke of Brittany, Constable of France, d. 1458.

Charles the Seventh: King of France, 1422-61.

Charlemagne: King of the Franks and Emperor of the West, d. 814.

the Scottish King: James II of Scotland, "known as 'the kyng of Scotts with the rede face.' . . . killed in 1460 by the explosion of a huge cannon while besieging Roxburgh Castle." (Bonner 195) The redness of his face was a birthmark.

And Cyprus, there's another one . . . : Jean III, King of Cyprus, d. 1458.

47. *Ladislaus*: Ladislaus of Bohemia, d. 1457.

Guesclin: Du Guesclin, Constable of France under Charles V, a hero of the Hundred Years' War, d. 1380.

Dauphin of Auvergne: Either Béraud II (+ 1400), Dauphin of Auvergne and Count of Clermont, or his son, d. 1426.

Duke of Alençon: Either Jean II, who was not yet dead when Villon wrote but had been condemned for treason and dispossessed of his lands and titles, or Jean I who died at the Battle of Agincourt in 1415. (Bonner)

ANOTHER BALLADE In Old French: Villon is attempting to write in the French of some 250 years past. Scholars of Old French have found his to be ungrammatical and "unsystematic."

Where is the Pope, His Holiness? The people mentioned in this ballade—pope, emperor, et al—are not particular individuals but types.

51. *The Beautiful Helmet Maker*: Although she is anonymous there was in fact a beautiful helmet maker (employee of an armorer). She was born about 1375 and became the mistress of Nicholas d'Orgement, financier, canon of Notre Dame, and brother of the Bishop of Paris. She is mentioned in the Cathedral register. Nicholas installed her in one of the cloisters of the Cathedral, against all church regulations. In 1416 he was involved in a plot against the king, tried by the chapter of Notre Dame, and condemned. His property was confiscated and he was imprisoned on "the bread of pain and water of anguish." The prison was that of the Bishop of Orléans at Mehun, where Villon would be imprisoned forty-five years later. If Villon is sticking to the facts, the beautiful Helmet Maker then consorted with a pimp who died around 1426. When Villon knew her, before he left Paris in 1456, she must have been about eighty.

Grieving for her youth that's gone: Maurice Allem comments (186): "An old woman regretting the happy times of her youth and frivolous loves is a commonplace of the poetry of the Middle Ages. M. Italo Siciliano (*F. Villon et les thèmes poétiques du moyen âge, p. 376*) has researched this theme from poet to poet, from the twelfth century to the century of Villon which, here again, has followed an old course. The Beautiful Helmet Maker in her old age resembles other deposed lovers, among them the old woman in the *Roman de la Rose* with whom she has many traits in common and the drama of a degrading love. But, as always, Villon has drawn these traits with a vigor, a truthfulness, a primitivism [*une crudité*], a cruelty, a brilliance that makes his portrait the most beautiful and impressive in this sad gallery."

53. *Where has the smooth forehead gone*: This itemization of ideal female beauty is a convention of medieval poetry, and so is the ideal ugliness. The items are described in descending order.

57. *Soon set aflame,/ And soon burned out*: Sargent-Baur comments (203): "If the brief flame symbolizes the brevity of beauty, it is one of the very rare symbols in Villon's poetry."

the daughters of joy: The Glove Girl, Blanche the Shoemaker, the Sausage Seller, Guillemette for Tapestry, the Bonnet Maker, and Catherine are shopgirls. Women like these hoped to augment their mean salaries by finding a "protector," a man who would support them. The Helmet Maker's advice to them is, "Grab all the money that you can." Some were frankly prostitutes—in any case, they had a shady reputation. The poet argues with a suppositious man who would say that these women have no morals and are only out for all they can get. He says, "Each had chosen with her heart," so their first love affairs were honest. But their subsequent behavior, as he describes it, is not so innocent. He hastens to say that he's not blaming them: "Love is so nice, they want to share."

61. *In accord with the Decree*: The Decree was a collection of rules by popes and church fathers made by Gratian, a monk of the twelfth century. Adultery was vigorously condemned; it was conceded, however, that the sin would be less if it were concealed. "Villon, we see, amuses himself by presenting this concession as though it were a prescription." (Maurice Allem 188) Sargent-Baur refers to the Mss. that say "ce decret,"and takes "ce" to be "a rather vague demonstrative"— "that rule (the one we all know about, the one we see followed)." (203) This reading strikes me as right. It is in Villon's familiar, off-hand manner.

63. *blind Samson*: Samson was betrayed by Delilah. She cut off his hair, the source of his strength, and he was blinded by the Philistines. (Judges 16:15-21)

Solomon/ With idols: Solomon was King of Israel in the tenth century B.C. He had 700 wives and 300 concubines: "his wives turned away his heart after other gods." (I Kings 11:3-4)

Cerberus: In Greek mythology, the *three-headed* dog at the entrance to the underworld. Orpheus had to pass it in order to retrieve his wife, Eurydice.

Narcissus: Villon makes Narcissus a lover of women, but the generally accepted story is that he was in love with his own image in a pool.

Sardanapulus: a king of Assyria.

King David: David, King of Israel, saw Bathsheba, the wife of Uriah, washing herself. He arranged for Uriah to be in the front line of battle and be killed. David then married Bathsheba. The Lord sent Nathan to David with a message—he would be punished: "the sword shall never depart from thy house." (II Samuel 12:10)

65. *Amnon:* Absalom, a son of David, had a "fair sister," Tamar. Another son of David, Amnon, was in love with Tamar. Amnon pretended to be sick, and asked to have Tamar make him some cakes and bring them to his chamber. There he raped her. Absalom waited to take his revenge; two years later he had Amnon killed. (II Samuel 13)

King Herod: In the first century Herod Antipas was tetrarch of Galilee. His stepdaughter Salome's dancing so pleased him that he swore that he would give her whatever she asked. Her mother Herodias hated John the Baptist for speaking against her marriage to Herod. She told Salome to ask for the Baptist's head, and Herod obliged her.

Now of myself: This "pleasant tale" is a surprise. The other stories are from legends and Scripture—this is taken from life and depicts a wedding scene like a genre painting. There was a de Vaucelles family near Saint Benoît where Villon lodged. The Noel who, together with Villon, gets beaten at the wedding may be the same Noel who is left 220 blows in his will. Apparently it was the custom for the wedding guests to lay about them, "to help them remember the occasion." (Sargent-Baur 204)

the man who rides a broom: A witch. Such men were burned alive.

67. *Take your lanterns and leave you bladders:* A proverbial saying.

69. *I can pick up my fiddle:* This is from another proverbial saying: "My fiddle is under the bench"—as we might say, "I've packed it in." I have changed the saying to a shout by a woman as she shows the poet the door: "You can pick up your fiddle!"

Most editions of the poem have "elles," the plural form of the pronoun, when Villon speaks of "Amours,"and we understand him to mean that love affairs in general have made him disillusioned. But in all the manuscripts it is "elle," the singular pronoun, which has led some commentators to say that he means the particular mistress he has been talking about who treated him so badly. I think there is no contradiction—the confusion of singular and plural in these stanzas is deliberate: Villon is envisioning both one woman and several. As the narrator envisions one woman and relives a scene, other women he has known come to mind, a chorus telling him to go to hell. The fugue is a masterpiece of narrative:

> I can pick up my fiddle by the exit
> As I leave. She wishes I would.
> I can go straight to hell. Understood?
> What, they ask, am I waiting for?

"Jacobins": Dominicans who wore gowns of white wool, therefore Villon can compare them to gobs of spit. His detestation of Mendicant friars we already know.

Jehanneton: Woman in general.

Tacque Thibault: Villon gives this name of a detested man to Thibault d'Aussigny, the Bishop of Orléans who held him in prison at Mehun-sur-Loire. Tacque Thibault was a shoemaker of the previous century who became a favorite of the Duke of Berry, from whom he received money and offices, and who made himself hated for his exactions and vile behavior. Here Villon recalls the tortures inflicted upon him in prison. The "bitter pear" was an iron gag used to prevent the prisoner undergoing torture from crying out. Villon calls it "the pear of anguish," a name it had been given because there was a pear in the village of Angoisse in Périgord that had a bitter taste.

71. *his prosecutor*: Pierre Bourgoin. His name is all that is known about him.

his judge: Etienne Plaisant, a doctor of law who would work his way up to be, after the death of Thibault d'Aussigny, Vicar General of the diocese. Plaisant is said to have been a harsh judge—which is why Villon says that he is, "for an official . . . pleasant enough."

Master Robert: This was the son of the hangman, and would be the hangman in his turn.

As Lombards adore/ Their God: Lombards were known as bankers, money changers, and usurers, all of whom were held in execration by God.

Provins, Moreau,/ Robin Turgis: Jean de Provins was a pastry cook in the rue du Chaume; Jean Moreau, a "roaster" who in May 1454 was made a master in his corporation; Robin Turgis, the host at the celebrated *Pine Cone Tavern* in the rue de la Juiverie, across from the Church of the Madeleine. For his heirs Villon has designated a pastry cook, a meat cook, and the owner of a tavern. It seems probable that he owed each of these men money, but he says they are in debt to him—they "have had their shares." His legacies to them are worthless, which is nearly always the case. He promises to pay Turgis what he owes him for wine, a payment Turgis may collect if he can find out Villon's address. But perhaps instead of paying him, he'll promise to make him a magistrate. He says that he is empowered to do this, for he was born in Paris (page 91).

73. *my clerk who's listening*: Favier says that the clerk Frémin was *un brave garçon*. This would have been Frémin le Lay, a notary public. The narrator will "put his pen under contribution" and pretend, without having any illusions, that he has a secretary in Frémin. (Favier 441)

none feels much heat: The patriarchs and prophets lived before Christianity and were not baptised, but the Church Fathers said that they were Christian believers by anticipation. Christ took them out of Hell—as Villon says, they weren't feeling much heat. (King Louis released Villon and the other prisoners at Mehun when he passed through. Monarchs would do this on occasion, following Christ's example. It was good public relations.)

What of the Virtuous Heathen who had not anticipated Christ's coming? They are not being torn by demons or subjected to fire or cold. They appear to be as they were in the world: they have dignity and honor. Gluck in his opera *Orpheus and Eurydice* has them moving in a stately dance. Dante places them in Limbo, a border of Hell. In Limbo there is a constant sound of sighing, for the pagans have desire without hope. Besides, they have to share the space with unbaptised infants.

75. *Lazarus*: The rich man would not let Lazarus have crumbs from his table when Lazarus was hungry. Though neither a patriarch nor prophet, Lazarus was transported to Paradise in Abraham's bosom. The rich man when he died went to Hell. He asked Abraham to let Lazarus give him water from the tip of his finger. Abraham refused. (Luke 16:26)

What is the relevance of this parable to Villon's argument? He has been accused of talking about theology though he doesn't have the credentials: "What authority/ Gives you the right to lecture us?" But does knowing a parable make you an authority on theology? Or does he see his critic as the rich man and himself as the beggar Lazarus? Also, the stricture against drunkenness that follows seems to have been lugged in just to be saying something—he has lost the thread of his narrative. Why is the poet who liked wine so much preaching against drunkenness? The sermon doesn't appear to be ironic, like W. C. Field's temperance lecture. It is time to return to his first idea...the legacies. And he does.

nine new orders of the sky: The nine choirs of angels.

77. *From dust it goes to dust*: "dust thou art, and unto dust shalt thou return." (Genesis 3:19)

"Wherefore then hast thou brought me forth?": Job 10:18. This line is not in Villon—I have inserted it in order to rhyme. Villon, who has just quoted the Bible and knows it well, might also have thought of this question—it follows naturally: if we are born of dust, and returning to dust, why are we born?

Master Guillaume de Villon: Villon's adoptive father, a chaplain and professor of canon law who had a house in the cloister of Saint Benoît.

Romance of the Farting Devil: We do not know whether, as has been surmised, this was a verse narrative written by Villon in his youth and lost. But we do know there was a big stone that was called The Farting Devil. It stood on the property of a Mademoiselle de Bruyères on the Right Bank. Students from the University used her stone as a picnic table and wrote their names on it. They carried it away to rue Mont Saint Hilaire, the student quarter. Parliament authorized the police lieutenant at the Châtelet to look into the matter and bring the stone to the Châtelet as evidence.

In the 1450s students frequently came into conflict with respectable citizens who objected to their dress, their attitudes, their behavior, everything that students have been known for from the fifteenth century to the present. Mademoiselle de Bruyères was very active in pious works, rehabilitating "fallen women"—no wonder she was a target for student pranks. (For more about her see page 119 and the note.)

Some of the clerks wore the tonsure and gown only in order to claim the privileges of the church. "The clerks," Champion says, "formed at the end of the Middle Ages the class *par excellence* of the corrupt and sometimes vagabond.... they diced, raped young women, sang in the evening in the streets, mocking songs or love songs, carried sticks, and played farces that sometimes turned to tragedy." (*I*, 65)

Guy Tabarie: One of the gang who robbed the College of Navarre. Villon calls him "homs veritable," a truthful man. He probably means that when Tabarie was arrested and questioned, that is, tortured, he talked.

79. *the Egyptian*: Mary, a prostitute of Alexandria who was converted to Christianity and lived in the desert.

Theophilus: He made a pact with the devil, repented, and was converted to Christianity.

At the church I belong to: This was the church of the monastery of the Celestins, on the right bank of the Seine, near the church of Saint Paul. Among the decorations were paintings of Hell and Paradise.

81. *my love, my dear rose*: The "rose" is his mistress. He is leaving her neither his heart nor his faith. He says that she has enough money... but she would like a big silk purse filled with coins. Since she doesn't want money, the purse must be male genitals. Coming after the prayer he has given his mother to speak, this brings us up short. We are reminded of the kind of man Villon is—not at all sentimental. He doesn't believe in romantic love—he speaks of the relations between men and women with a realism that can be bitter. As for his faith, his idea of heaven wouldn't be like his mother's, a place where harps and lutes are playing—it would be like the Pine Cone Tavern. Hell isn't a mural painted on a church wall, but the wall to which he has been chained.

Michault: Bonner comments that if Michaud (sic) ever existed, "he quickly passed into legend." In a poem, *Contrefait de Renart*

(1328), the wife of Ysengrin the wolf says that she would like to be reborn as a man: "There wouldn't be one woman I'd spare."

Saint Satur, beneath Sancerre: There is a Saint Satur near a hill named Sancerre, but no evidence of a connection with Michault. Apparently the name Satur made Villon think of Michault who had the sexual appetite of a satyr.

83. *Pernet with the Bar*: Perrenet Marchand. He has already been mentioned twice: in *The Legacy* on page 13, *The Testament* on page 70.

85. *Ythier Marchant*: Mentioned in *The Legacy* on page 7 where the narrator bequeaths him his *branc* (sword or excrement or erect penis). Bonner comments that Marchant didn't set the lay to music, but someone else did, "a composer of considerable talent. The piece is best performed with voice and two instruments, and it should be remembered that the first verse is repeated in its entirety at the end." (199)

87. *Master Jehan Cornu*: He was named with Marchant in *The Legacy* as an alternative heir of the narrator's *branc*. Here Villon leaves him Bobignon's garden. Pierre Bobignon or Baubignon was a lawyer attached to the Châtelet. It seems that he was supposed to be fixing up some gardens to pay a debt. We can speculate about the house with the missing door that the narrator says he rented from Bobignon. Was he squatting in the house? Were the ten falcons so many thieves, his associates? The hoe handle and paving stone could have been used in fights. The hook he speaks of may have been a burglar's tool. And so on.

the wife/ Of Master Pierre Amant: Villon detests her because she said he was "indigent." *The White Horse* and *The She-Mule* are tavern signs. Perhaps he is bequeathing to Pierre Saint Amant (*The White Horse*) who is impotent (stands still) a wife who will be different from the one he now has, and to his sterile wife (*The She-Mule*) a "red ass." In another place Villon speaks of "the ass's game," and there it definitely means copulating (page 123). But there has been no satisfactory explanation of these lines.

Sire Denis/ Hesselin: a fiscal judge in charge of tax legislation. Apparently he drinks.

Turgis: the owner of the *Pine Cone Tavern*.

89. *Master Guillaume Charruau*: He has not been identified. For

Marchant, see *The Legacy*, page 7 and the note for that page. A *rëau* was a coin, but it could be pronounced *rot*, meaning a belch. The Temple was an enclosed area in London belonging to the Order of the Knights Templar. Villon follows this stanza with a legacy to his lawyer, and as lawyers live in the Temple today, I think they may have frequented it then. There would have been many occasions when the Knights needed a lawyer.

Fournier: See *The Legacy*, page 11 and note.

Jacques/ Raguier: See *The Legacy*, page 11 and note. *Plaques* were coins of little value. The word also means scabs.

Merebeuf/ and Nicolas de Louviers: See *The Legacy*, page 18 and note. They had pretensions as landed gentry. Villon is saying that they would be more capable of raising poultry.

91. *Robin Turgis*: He has already been mentioned twice (*The Testament*, pages 70 and 86). If you were born in Paris you could be a city magistrate, but this didn't give you the right to make someone a magistrate. This legacy has no value. Villon says, *"je parle ung peu poictevin,"* "I am speaking with a somewhat Pouitou accent," which meant to deceive or deny.

The slight accent: The lines that follow are in an accent of the south. Some translators have tried to render them in a Dixie accent. Sargent-Baur comments (211) that Saint Générou and Saint Julien de Voventes are 100 kilometers apart. "It has been suggested that these place-names hide double meanings, directed at Turgis: Generou [sic], in Parisian pronunciation, was Genescou (= *je ne soulds*, 'I don't pay'), and Voventes supplied the direct object (*vos ventes*, 'your sales, what you've sold me')."

Sergeant Jehan Raguier: Also mentioned in *The Legacy*, page 11 and note.

Bailly: Jean de Bailly, a clerk at the Treasury. His house was next to the *Maubué* fountain.

Prince of Fools: The Prince of Fools was in charge of public entertainments. Also see *The Legacy*, page 19 and note.

Michault du Four: A police officer at the Châtelet who helped in the investigation of the robbery at the College of Navarre. He was frequently involved in quarrels and litigation. (Champion *II*, 336-337).

93. *Denis Richier and Jehan Vallette*: Two of the Guards, the foot patrol of the Paris police, commanded by the Provost. Villon gives

each of the Guards "une grant cornete," which I have translated as "strip of velvet." The strip was attached to the hat and fell to the shoulder. The word suggests *cornette de chanvre*, "hemp," that is, a rope. (Sargent-Baur) There were 200 men in the foot patrol, and also mounted Guards who patroled outside the city.

Perrenet: See *The Legacy*, page 13 and note.

Cholet: The river policeman who was also, among other things, a barrel maker. See *The Legacy*, page 13, where Loup and Cholet are stealing coal and firewood from the boats they are supposed to be guarding.

Jehan le Lou: This would be the Loup mentioned along with Cholet in *The Legacy*, page 13.

95. *de Bois the Goldsmith*: Jean Mahé, a guard at the Châtelet. He is on record as being one of the five who, in 1476, tortured the Duke of Nemours. Ginger was thought to be an aphrodisiac, and so were spices from the East such as "Saracen cloves."

Captain Jehan Riou: Captain of the municipal guard, 120 archers who appeared on ceremonial occasions. He was also a dealer in skins.

Six wolf heads: An unlikely dish. Sargent-Baur, by oral permission, speaks of "an elaborate play of allusions" which, in this and the next stanza, make "a threatening bequest: for 'toy soldiers,' real criminals and real warfare."

Robinet Trascaille: a clerk at the Treasury.

97. *Perrot Girart*: He has not been identified.

Filles Dieu and Beguines: See *The Legacy*, page 17 and note.

Turlupins and Turlupines: People of Flanders who had been declared heretics. They appear to have been Rousseauists before Rousseau: they believed in the goodness of nature, went in for nudism, and were, naturally, said to be dissolute.

Jehan de Poullieu: A theologian at the University of Paris in the early thirteenth century. He preached and wrote against Mendicant friars' being allowed to hear confession. Pope John XXII ordered him to make a public retraction. I have not included *et reliqua* in my translation: it means "all the rest."

Jehan de Mehun: Author of the second part of *Roman de la Rose*. (c. 1275 A.D.) He has False Seeming say, "I dwell in religion only to trick people."

Matheolus: Author of *Liber lamentationum*, in which he attacks the Mendicants. The work was translated into French in the 1370s.

99. *Brother Baude*: Baude de la Mare, a Carmelite. Villon has just said that he won't speak against them again . . . and proceeds to do so.

halberd: A battle axe and pike on a handle six feet long.

sallet: A light helmet without a visor and with a projection over the neck.

Detusca: Sargent-Baur suggests Jean Turquant, an officer of the Provost of Paris.

green cage: A symbol of the female. The color green implied fickleness and promiscuity.

Vauvert's devil: Vauvert was an old royal residence outside Paris that was given to the Carthusians in the13th century. It was said to be inhabited by demons, possibly because it was near the old Porte de l'Enfer, Gate of Hell. (Sargent-Baur)

Keeper of the Seal: Le Seelleur=Richard de la Palu. Villon says that he chewed beeswax to soften it so that it would take the imprint of the seal. Surely this is a joke.

If he has a fit?: I have changed Villon's words here, for the reason given before, to keep the form of his verse. The word *Eveschié* that Villon uses and I have not included means "Official." I don't think anything has been lost.

gentlemen auditors: Clerks of the Accounting Office. It seems they were envious of the wood paneling in the High Court.

Macee: Macé d'Orléans, a judge. Perhaps Villon's contemporaries knew why he has made Macé female and a slut.

101. *Master Françoys*: Françoys de la Vacquerie, an ecclesiastical prosecutor. Champion says he "did not have an easy character"— apparently he was a brawler. (*II*, 340-341) Candidates for knighthood were given a blow, but as a man of the church de la Vacquerie was not a candidate for knighthood. The reference is probably to a beating he received.

Jehan Laurens: A prosecutor of the Paris diocese. He obtained the confession from Guy Tabarie that implicated Villon in the robbery of the College of Navarre.

Bourges: Jean Coeur, Archbishop of Bourges, son of Jacques Coeur the wealthy businessman. See page 39 and note.

Jehan Cotart: Another diocesan prosecutor. He defended Villon in court, and the poet clearly has a great deal of affection for him. Cotart died on January 9, 1461.

Denise: Unknown.

Father Noah: Genesis 9:20-21.

Lot: Genesis 19:30-36.

103. *Architriclinus*: Master of the feast at Cana of Galilee where Christ turned water into wine. This was His first miracle. (John 2:3-11)

Merle: Germain de Marle, a money-changer.

105. *three poor little orphans*: The three old men we've heard about in *The Legacy* on page 15.

Salins: A city in the Jura, named after the salt works there. Sargent-Baur comments that "one source of the wealth of the 'orphans' was their speculation in the salt trade." (215)

Order of the Mathurins: Saint Mathurin was invoked to cure madness. He is probably mentioned here because the next stanza recommends not over-taxing one's brains with study.

Pierre Richier: A master of theology who taught children.

Donat's: The *Donatus* was the Latin grammar used in schools. Villon is punning on the verb "*donner*," to give: the *Donat*, giving, would be too hard for the "orphans" to learn. Instead, have them taught how to make money. These three, however, wouldn't have needed the instruction.

Ave salus, tibi decus: The Latin is a parody of a Latin hymn to the Virgin. "Saluts" and "écus" were gold coins. The line may be translated, "Hail saluts, glory to thee, écus!" Bonner comments, "One could even go one pun further." *Decus* sounds like *des culs*, that is, arses.

Credo: "I believe," the confession of faith that is still said in church. It also means, "I give credit." The "orphans" would be very unwilling to give it.

I'll tear my long coat in two: Saint Martin of Tours, a bishop of the fourth century, divided his cloak with a beggar.

pies: The word "flans" also meant the metal disks used for minting money. (Bonner)

107. *my clerks*: See *The Legacy*, page 15 and note.

Gueuldry Guillaume: See *The Legacy*, page 15 and note.

College Clerk: The College of the Eighteen Clerks, one of the oldest in Paris, had a bad reputation: it had been called "not a college but a den of thieves." (Bonner 116) *collator*: A man who dispensed an ecclesiastical benefice. Collators would be old men, so it wouldn't be likely that the narrator had met their mothers.

109. *Michault Cul d'Oue . . . Charlot Taranne*: Rich money-changers. "To put on the boot" meant to have sexual intercourse.

Lord of Grigny: Philippe Brunel. See *The Legacy*, page 11 and note. The tower of Billy was another ruin. The tower was sequestered by the court: there was a lawsuit between a man who claimed to have a lease on it for life and the Celestins who claimed ownership. Bonner comments, "a fine gift for the cantankerous old Brunel."

Thibault de la Garde . . . Jehan de la Garde: See *The Legacy*, page 15 and note. Both these names were synonyms of "cuckold."

The Wine Cask: Le Barillet, a tavern.

Genevoys: Pierre Genevoys, an attorney at the Châtelet. "Dufournet conjectures that he had a red nose, sign of a serious drinker." (Sargent-Baur 216)

Basennier . . . Mautaint: See *The Legacy*, page 11 and note. *Jehan de Ruel* was an auditor at the Châtelet whose brother was a grocer, so that Ruel was authorized to receive spices given in payment. Nicolas *Rosnel* was an examiner at the Châtelet. "All four men . . . were under the authority of the *prévôt* (chief of police)." (Sargent-Baur 216)

The lord who serves Saint Christopher: Robert d'Estouteville, the Provost and Chief of Police who protected Villon to some extent. Villon's references to this man are unctuous, and the ballade supposed to be spoken by d'Estouteville to his wife is stomach-turning. He tells her that he is going to have intercourse with her because it is his duty to God.

111. *Hector or Troilus*: Warriors in the Trojan War.

Everyone who's married does. It's the reason. D'Estouteville is some centuries before his time—he could be an Englishman living in the reign of Victoria. Bonner comments (211): "The details about his winning his wife at a tournament are historic fact. At Saumur in 1446, René d'Anjou, King of Sicily, held a *pas d'armes* with forty days of tournaments at which Robert d'Estouteville turned up armed almost like a character in a Sir Walter Scott novel, with a turbaned Moor's head as a crest on his helmet and a horse draped in azure cloth."

113. *Perdriers*: Jean and Françoys Perdrier held administrative of-

fices in Paris. Françoys was licensed to sell fish, and may have served the royal table. (Champion *II*, 314-318)

Bruges: What's the significance of red tongue in Bruges? No one seems to know. Perhaps the younger Françoys means that Villon's tongue is as peppery as the kind of tongue they cook in Bruges. So he should take it there.

Taillevent: Guillaume Tirel. In the fourteenth century he wrote a cookbook, the *Viandier*, that was very popular, the *Joy of Cooking* of its day.

Macquaire: Legendary as a bad cook. Bonner suggests that Villon may also have had in mind "Saint Macaire of *The Golden Legend* who had power over demons."

In arsenic from pulverized rock: This ballade is a *sotte chanson,* a composition that was deliberately satiric, coarse, and, my book says, disgusting.

115. *Andry Courault*: Royal counselor at the Treasury and legal adviser to King René d'Anjou (the same who held the tournament at which d'Estouteville shone). In 1454 the King composed a pastoral, *Regnault et Jehanneton*, idealizing the love of a shepherd and shepherdess. Courault was a neighbor of Villon in Paris: he lived in rue Saint Jacques, near Saint Benoît. Bonner remarks that Courault "apparently had been of no help in obtaining René d'Anjou's patronage for the poet." (210) In 1462 he represented Bishop Thibault d'Aussigny. (Champion *II*, 312-313)

Franc Gontier: The hero of a poem by the forteenth century poet, Philippe de Vitry. Gontier and his wife Helaine live by their labor on the land and have no possessions, but they are free and happy.

the tyrant: Pierre d'Ailly, a chancellor of the University of Paris, wrote a poem in which he contrasted Gontier's life with that of a rich tyrant. The tyrant with his castle, sumptuous feasts, lechery, and avarice, is melancholy. Gontier's simple life is much to be preferred.

the sage: Solomon. He was thought to be the author of Ecclesiastes. The paraphrase by Villon is from Ecclesiasticus 8:1-2: "Strive not with a powerful man, lest thou fall into his hands. Contend not with a rich man, lest he bring an action against thee."

117. *My Lady Sidoine*: Perhaps named after the heroine of a late fourteenth or early fifteenth century prose romance, *Ponthus et la belle Sidoyne*. Villon specifies that the lovers are drinking "ypocras"—

"a hot wine to which had been added sugar, cinnamon, ginger and pepper and which was considered a strong aphrodisiac." (Bonner 210-211)

With a couch nearby?: Villon says, "Lequel vault mieux? Lict costoyé de chaise?" Maurice Allem says that he cannot make sense of this expression, and the construction of the question is puzzling. Perhaps Villon is saying, is it better to lie under a rose bush when you might be lying on a couch?

119. *Mademoiselle de Bruyères*: Catherine de Bruyères was a widow, sixty-nine years old, when Villon was writing *The Testament*. She was very devout: she gave money to the Carmelites and went about rehabilitating "fallen women." She had a following of young, unmarried women, and they preached in the Linen Market where lingerie was sold, not far from Les Halles. The only women allowed to work in the market were servants whose mistresses vouched that they had a good reputation. If one of these women misbehaved she would be admonished. If she persisted, she would be banned from the market by the assembly of mistresses. These lost sheep would be brought back to the path of righteousness by the preaching of Catherine de Bruyères and her young women—but Allem remarks that there would be times when the lost sheep would express themselves with the repartees "such women knew how to make." When Villon says that de Bruyères and her associates shouldn't preach in the graveyard he may be thinking of the Cemetery of the Innocents in the Les Halles quarter. The cemetery was used for preaching, and the Linen Market was held outside it on certain days. The cemetery was also frequented by prostitutes.

121. *Macrobius*: Latin grammarian and philosopher, c. A.D. 400. His works were still in the university curriculum. The second book of his *Saturnalia* mainly consists of witticisms: this was probably the work that was best known by students.

Montmartre's mount: There was a convent on the hill of Montmartre. The buildings were in ruins, and the few nuns still living there sold wine.

Mount Valerien: A hill to the west of Paris on which there was a small hermitage. Sargent-Baur comments (222), "Villon seems to be 'moving mountains,' but is really playing with words (Valerien=valent rien, 'are worth nothing')."

the pardon/I brought from Rome: Villon had never been in Rome, and as the nuns were selling wine out of the convent, a pardon (three-month indulgence) would have been worth nothing.

123. *Jacobins*: Dominicans. See page 69 and note.

Jacqueline and Perrete,/And Ysabeau: Just names. No women have been identified to go with them.

"By the Lord, bigod!": Villon has "Enné!" Sargent-Baur says that this is "an exclamation, seemingly used by women more than by men." Like "Dear me!" I suppose. But I have made it stronger, bringing up the English "bigod" from the next stanza, for the women are discussing friars who get the goodies these women would like to have. Until 1436 Paris was under the domination of the English. They were said to be devils who would cut the throat of a Christian they caught outside the city walls. The occupying army spread its oaths around, and the French, especially the prostitutes, picked them up. I have added a "begad," also English (P. G. Wodehouse's kind) for the rhyme.

Fat Margot: There may have been a "historical" Margot, but Champion says that Margot was a generic name for a prostitute. (Champion I, 109) "The "Ballade of Fat Margot" is a *sotte chanson*—satiric, and the coarseness is deliberate. There is nothing attractive about the picture the speaker gives of his life, nothing self-flattering: "We love filth, and so filth follows us./ We fly from honor, and honor abhors us..."

125. *Bene stat*: "It stands well."

"Gogo" : "Margot, 'laughing,' gives us a fine specimen of the so expressive and inarticulate onomatopoeia of children: 'Gogo' she says..." (Mus 32-33)

127. *Marion l'Idolle/ And tall Jehanne*: Prostitutes. Marion l'Idolle is documented. (Champion *I*, 111-113)

prison at Mehun: Where Villon was incarcerated in the summer of 1461.

Noel Jolis: Perhaps the same Noel who was knocked about at the wedding. See page 65.

At Henry's hands: Henry Cousin, the executioner in Paris, torturer and hangman.

Ostel/ Dieu: the city hospital.

Colin Galerne: "Galerne" means a cold wind from the north-west.

Besides being a barber Colin Galerne was a churchwarden and scribe. Barbers would do minor surgery—a man wounded in a street fight would be taken to a barber to be patched up. Galerne became assistant to the King's master barber. If he keeps the ice Villon is leaving him close to his chest he'll have pneumonia and be in a warm place next summer.

d'Angelot: Angelot Baugis. Both barber and herbalist were practicing medicine as it was known at the time.

129. *the Foundlings*: There was a foundling home in the Cité, run by the Cathedral.

the Lost Ones: Such as the "fallen women" to whom Mademoiselle de Bruyères and her cohorts preached. They should be living with the prostitute Marion l'Idolle.

a garland: On festive occasions men would wear a garland of flowers on their head.

Montpipeau: A fortress near Mehun-sur-Loire. Villon is punning: *aller piper* meant to trick, to cheat at dice.

Rueil: A place west of Paris with which Villon has the same wordplay: *aller ruer* meant to strike down.

Colin de Cayeux: One of Villon's associates in the robbery of the College of Navarre. He was the son of a locksmith, and one of the two who picked the lock of the strongbox in which the gold écus were held. He also took part in a robbery of the church of the Augustines. He had to leave Paris, then he operated in Normandy. He was jailed several times but used his knowledge of locks to escape. He wore his clerical habit and tonsure so that he would not be arrested, but he was caught finally at Senlis. He appealed as a cleric, and two bishops supported his appeal, but he was condemned by a secular court to be "hanged and strangled." And so he was, on September 26, 1460.

the Queen of Carthage: Dido, in Virgil's *Aeneid*, a beautiful and passionate woman.

131. *peddling a new bull*: selling a fake indulgence. A bull was a document with the papal seal set in metal (*bulla*). Forgeries were common, especially of indulgences.

the kind they boil/ In oil: This seems an extraordinarily cruel punishment, but counterfeiting encroached on one of the fundamental rights of the king. Dante places falsifiers of the currency in Canto

XXX of the *Inferno*, near the bottom. Counterfeiting destroys the trust on which human society rests.

Playing in a village or a town: The church frowned on play-acting.

133. *that turns the body black*: If it has been left exposed on a gibbet, as hanged men were for the edification of the public.

the Fifteen Score: The Quinze Vings, a hospice for the blind.

Provins: 85 kilometers south-east of Paris. Provins had some connection with the Quinze Vings, but this is obscure.

At the Innocents: The Cemetery of the Innocents was the oldest cemetery in Paris. There were eighty arcades with two levels. Bones were piled on the upper arcade to make room for more recent burials, and exposed to public view.

135. *Of the King's Household*: Villon covers both ends of society, from the lord to the humble laborer. In the pile of skulls you couldn't tell one from the other.

I want the benefits extended: Sargent-Baur says that in extending absolution to the living who are opposed to avarice Villon is being heavily sarcastic. (226) The sarcasm is certainly heavy, for there is no way to tell what he thinks from the passage itself. But we can be sure that Villon doesn't think that officials are wearing themselves out in the service of the public.

God and Saint Dominic embrace: One day the administrators of justice will themselves have to appear before God and Saint Dominic to be judged.

137. *Jacquet Cardon*: See *The Legacy*, page 9 and note.

to fetch the mustard: Children were sent to buy freshly ground mustard and sang on the way. "Marionette" and "Open your door, Guillemette" were popular songs. "Not all of the songs," Sargent-Baur remarks, "were particularly suitable for children." Bonner says that mustard "had a second meaning which can be gleaned from these lines about a lover making fun of his lady. . . .

> You've ground your mustard in so many places
> That your mortar is no good any more."

On my return from prison: The prison at Mehun-sur-Loire. Sargent-Baur says that it is hard to know what to make of this rondeau, which is elevated in tone but has been introduced in an "offhand, if not obscene, manner." (226) But *The Testament* does not follow a settled order—the narrator seems to be talking of matters as they occur to him. Disjunction is to be expected of a character with a life such as François Villon's. Places, people drift in and out. He writes spontaneously as he talks. The prison at Mehun is never far from his mind.

Master Lomer: Pierre Lomer d'Airaines, a priest of the chapter of Notre Dame, was assigned to drive prostitutes out of the Ile de la Cité. Villon suggests that he was having intercourse with them.

the Tireless Dane: Ogier the Dane was a character in *chansons de geste*, but not in the role assigned to him here. Sargent-Baur suggests that Villon is confusing him with Oliver in the comic epic *Le Voyage de Charlemagne à Jerusalem et à Constantinople* who brags that he will make love to the Greek emperor's daughter a hundred times in a night.

Alain Chartier's legacy: Chartier was a royal secretary and the author of a poem in dialogue, "La Belle Dame sans Mercy," that was widely read. He leaves sick lovers to make songs, ditties and ballades. (Bonner, 213)

139. *Master Jacques James*: He owned several houses and a bathhouse. Some bathhouses were used as brothels, which may be why Villon says that he "shall be affianced to/ many women, but marry none."

the Seneschal: Perhaps Pierre de Brézé, Grand Seneschal of Normandy, who was imprisoned at Loches. Bonner says that he was "one of the finest soldiers and knights of the fifteenth century. He served Charles VII well, and as a result was imprisoned by Louis XI upon his accession to the throne." (214)

Chevalier du Guet: See *the Captain of the Watch* in *The Legacy*, page 13 and note.

Philebert and Fat Marquet: Unknown. They probably weren't so pretty.

Chappelain: He wasn't a clergyman but one of the twelve-man guard at the Châtelet. The joke is his name.

141. *Jehan de Calais*: There were several men with this name, but this Jehan de Calais must be the notary at the Châtelet who verified the legality of wills. Chappelain is the last individual named in *The Testament* to receive a bequest. Calais's services are now required to review the document and see that it is legally sound.

Sainte Avoye: A convent of Augustinian nuns in the rue du Temple, hardly the place to bury a poet with a reputation such as Villon's. Indoor burials were in a church or chapel, but this chapel was on the second floor and, as Villon says, this could not support a tomb.

a full-length picture: Many in their will specified that they wanted a sculpture or bronze effigy on their tomb. Villon wants a sketch.

145. *I would have it sounded*: The bell is La Jacqueline, the biggest of the bells in the tower of Notre Dame. It has cracked, been repaired, and recast in 1451. (It will be broken again in 1479.) So La Jacqueline is fragile. The manuscripts say "made of glass," but Clement Marot's edition of 1533 said "not made of glass," and this would be reprinted by most editors. Maurice Allem's text, which I am following, has the bell made of glass. (236-237) I like this much better.

Four loaves: The bell ringers were usually remembered in making a will. These rich men will pay the bell ringers for the sake of Saint Stephen. He was killed by stoning, so they will pay the ringers with stones.

Vollant: Guillaume Volant, a very rich man in the salt trade.

Jehan de la Garde: The grocer, another rich man. See *The Legacy*, page 19 and note.

Martin Bellefay: (Bellefoye) An officer on the Provost's staff.

Colombel: Guillaume Colombel, a rich landlord, moneylender, and royal secretary.

Michiel Jouvenel: A rich property owner and financier, employed in the royal household.

147. *In case they beg to be excused*: These rich and important men wouldn't go to the trouble of adminstering the estate of a nonentity like François Villon.

Philippe Brunel: (Philippe, Seigneur de Grigny) See *The Legacy*, page 11 and note; also *The Testament*, page 108 and note.

Jacques Raguier: See *The Legacy*, page 11 and note; also *The Testament*, page 91 and note.

Jacques James: See *The Testament*, page 139 and note. Sargent-Baur comments that the three alternative executors are very different from the narrator's first choices. They were men of standing in the community—he is being very ironic when he says that Brunel, Raguier, and James are honorable gentlemen and men of property.

Of course they would want no controller looking on if they were to administer his estate.

neither quid *nor* quod: Nothing at all.

Thomas Tricot: A priest of the diocese of Meaux, Villon's junior by three years.

Trou Perrete: Le Trou Perrecte, an indoor court where *jeu de paume*, an early form of tennis, was played. It was on the Ile de la Cité, opposite the Pine Cone Tavern. "But *tripot* also had an erotic sense, which Villon seems to be exploiting here." (Sargent-Baur 230)

Guillaume du Ru: He sold wine wholesale. Wine was sometimes referred to as oil. At the speaker's funeral oil will be needed for the lanterns, that is, wine.

149. *fawn boots*: It was a young man's fashion to wear *one* boot of this color. It was narrow and uncomfortable.

dogs who like to bite: Keepers of the prison at Mehun, Bishop Thibault d'Aussigny's hell hounds.

151. *ANOTHER BALLADE*: Someone else is speaking. The testator is dead but not yet buried, and we're invited to the funeral.

robed in red: "Red is the color of liturgical hangings and vestments when the feasts of martyrs are celebrated." (Sargent-Baur 230)

There wasn't a bush that didn't have on/ A bit of rag: In popular speech *brosse*, here translated as bush, meant "penis," and *lambeau*, which I have translated "rag," could refer to a bit of either cloth or flesh.

A martyr to love, as he swore/ On one testicle as he passed on: When a man made a testament he placed his hand on his testicles. If François swore on one testicle he was holding something back. "The witness [to the deathbed] will add one more exploit to his account:

> And that's not all. Love with his knife
> Gave him a stab as he lay dying.
> This pain, he said, was more trying
> Than a belt buckle. A metaphor?

The pun on *mallement*, brutally, or 'like a man' (*mâle*=the male sex) perfectly expresses the two functions of the 'martyr to love': to hunt and be hunted. This will prevent us from being deceived about the equivocal sense of the episode. Poor Villon as he lies dying is excited *in extremis,* his poor worn out male member once more begins the most splendid erection. This surpasses all measure, and the one who witnesses it will surpass himself if he enters into the spirit of the scene where his hero is rendering up his spirit." (Mus 333)

pichet: The smaller pitcher of wine, about two glasses, served in Paris to those who want to keep a clear head, for they hope to get some work done this afternoon.